D0606999

The Manipulators

THE MANIPULATORS

Facebook, Google, Twitter, and Big Tech's War on Conservatives

PETER J. HASSON

REGNERY
PUBLISHING
A Division of Salem Media Group

Regnery® is a registered trademark of Salem Communications Holding Corporation

ISBN 978-1-62157-958-8
ebook ISBN 978-1-62157-966-3
LCCN: 2019955220

Published in the United States by
Regnery Publishing
A Division of Salem Media Group
300 New Jersey Ave NW
Washington, DC 20001
www.Regnery.com

Manufactured in the United States of America

10 9 8 7 6 5 4 3 2 1

Books are available in quantity for promotional or premium use. For information on discounts and terms, please visit our website: www.Regnery.com.

To my parents, Seamus and Mary Hasson

CONTENTS

CHAPTER ONE

The Establishment vs. Free Speech

In June 1998, Matt Drudge announced in a speech to the National Press Club: "We have entered an era vibrating with the din of small voices. Every citizen can be a reporter, can take on the powers that be. The difference between the Internet, television and radio, magazines, newspapers, is the two-way communication. The Net gives as much voice to a [onetime] thirteen-year-old computer geek like me as to a CEO or speaker of the House. We all become equal. And you would be amazed what the ordinary guy knows."[1]

Less than five months earlier, Drudge had single-handedly sent the political and media worlds into turmoil. His website, the Drudge Report, not only broke the story of President Bill Clinton's affair with a White House intern, Monica Lewinsky, but revealed that *Newsweek* magazine had been sitting on the story. In one fell swoop, Drudge delivered a shattering blow to both the political and media establishments. That, Drudge reflected in June, was the power of the Internet: one man and a laptop could expose facts that important people wanted ignored.

Six years before Facebook was founded, seven years before Google launched YouTube, and eight years before Twitter existed, Drudge predicted the effect that platforms like theirs would have on public knowledge and the media industry. "And time was only newsrooms had access to the full pictures of the day's events. But now any citizen does. We get to see the kinds of cuts that are made for all kinds of reasons—endless layers of editors with endless agendas changing bits and pieces, so by the time the newspaper hits your welcome mat it had no meaning. Now, with a modem, anyone can follow the world and report on the world—no middleman, no Big Brother. And I guess this changes everything."

On October 13, 2016, eighteen years after Drudge's comments, legal scholar Jeffrey Rosen, in a speech at the Harvard Kennedy School of Government, delivered a prescient warning about the "most urgent free speech question of our time." That question, Rosen said, is how to "protect First Amendment values in an age where . . . young lawyers at Google and Facebook and Twitter have more power over who can speak . . . [and] be heard, than any king, or president, or Supreme Court justice." Rosen warned that Google, Facebook, and Twitter were facing "growing public pressure, here in America and around the world, to favor values such as dignity and safety rather than liberty and free expression" on their platforms.[2] As a result, the great challenge would be "to ensure that the American free speech tradition—which is so necessary for the survival of American democracy—flourishes online, rather than atrophying."

Rosen's "great concern," he told his audience, was that he was "not confident that the public will demand First Amendment and constitutional values—such as transparency, procedural regularity, and free expression—over dignity and civility. In colleges in America, and on digital platforms around the world, public pressure is clamoring in the opposite direction, in favor of dignity rather than liberty of thought and opinion." His speech centered on an ominous prediction of the future:

> As public pressures on the companies grow, they may increasingly try to abdicate their role as deciders entirely, to avoid being criticized for making unpopular decisions. I can imagine a future where Google, Twitter, and Facebook delegate their content decisions to government, to users, or even to popular referenda, in order to avoid criticism and accountability for exercising human judgment. The result would be far more suppression of speech, and less democratic deliberation than exists now, making the age of the deciders look like a brief shining age, a Periclean oasis before the rule of the mob with a dictator.

Rosen's pessimistic vision didn't take long to become reality.

Donald Trump's election in 2016 sent a shockwave through the liberal political and media establishment. That establishment suddenly realized that it had lost control of the national conversation. Panicked, it turned to Big Tech to censor and suppress open debate on the Internet in order to control it and bring it in line with the left-liberal consensus of the media, the Democratic Party, and public education, which has long been hostile to "politically incorrect" thinking and speech.

If they succeed, it will be bad news for people who believe in freedom and diversity of opinion, because the mainstream media, the Democratic Party, and the education establishment are among the most intellectually narrow-minded institutions in American life. Even the *Washington Post* has acknowledged that "liberal intolerance is on the rise on America's college campuses, with data showing that college students have steadily become more intolerant of controversial speech in the last half century.[3] Although the average American is more likely to be a self-described conservative than a self-described liberal, left-leaning professors outnumber conservative professors in academia more than five-to-one.[4] Ten times as many professors are registered Democrats than are registered Republicans.[5] Public school teachers, many of whom graduate from left-wing schools of education, are also overwhelmingly on the left.[6]

Viewpoint diversity is no greater within the media: most every cable news program slants leftward. (In fact, Fox News tops the cable news ratings precisely because it's the only major network that speaks to the right side of the aisle.) A 2014 study found that between 2002 and 2013, the percentage of mainstream journalists who were registered Republicans fell from 18 percent to 7 percent.[7] Other studies confirm that the average journalist is much more likely to be left-wing than the average American.[8]

The left's stranglehold on education and media has serious consequences for the lives of everyday Americans. It's how ideas like "toxic masculinity," "white privilege," and "preferred pronouns," leak into mainstream discourse: they germinate in the offices of far-left academics, migrate to the news and editorial desks at the *New York Times*, buzz into the minds of Democratic politicians, and then are stamped into the mandatory curriculum at your local high school. Of course, not every journalist or public school teacher is a leftist, but the data make clear that most are, especially at the upper levels of their professions. The power players in these industries are all on the same ideological team, and they are all part of the same liberal establishment that has driven America's national discourse for decades.

The advent of Internet search engines like Google, video-hosting sites like YouTube, and social media platforms like Facebook and Twitter, produced new ways around the left's information monopoly; they empowered private citizens to report events, express opinions, and reach broad audiences on a scale that had traditionally been reserved for network news anchors, print reporters, and prominent intellectuals.

Social media represents a real threat to the political monoculture enforced by elite institutions. Absent an editorial tilt, social media is pure democracy. That's why social media, more than any other medium, is where conservatives have gained their strongest foothold, and it's also precisely why the progressive left feels the need to censor online speech so urgently.

CNN commentator Kirsten Powers, herself a liberal, confessed that seen through the "narrow and intolerant lens" of people on the "illiberal left," "disagreement is violence. Offending them is akin to physical assault. They are so isolated from the marketplace of ideas, that when confronted with a view they don't like, they feel justified in doing whatever they can to silence that speech."[9]

That's why there's a push on many university campuses—where the illiberal left dominates—to make "microaggressions" reportable to the campus police department. It's also the premise upon which left-wing agitators try to shut down Chick-fil-A franchises because the company's owner supports traditional marriage. And that's how you get New York City Mayor Bill de Blasio boycotting Chick-fil-A after it opened a franchise that provided jobs in his city.[10]

At the ideological heart of the left today is the theory of intersectionality, which holds that interlocking systems of oppression determine most of the world's outcomes. White women are victims, but less so than black men, who themselves are less marginalized than black women, who have more privilege than black transgender women, and so on. The more boxes you check that identify you as a member of a marginalized group, the more oppressed you are. And the more oppressed you are, the more deference your views should receive. Individuals who are more "intersectional" have a greater right to speak than those who score lower on the intersectionality scale.

If your goal was to create the opposite of a self-help philosophy, you'd land on intersectionality. The way to change your life for the better isn't to work hard, practice good habits and make good decisions—the way to change your life is to overthrow the systems of oppression that are keeping you down, and the way to gain moral authority among your peers is to achieve a higher level of victimhood. Because all oppressions are interlinked, the way to solve an issue is to chop away at our capitalist, racist, misogynistic system, no matter how narrow your concern may be. Once you overthrow the system, then your life can improve. As *New York Magazine*'s Andrew Sullivan observes, intersectionality has a quasi-religious element to it that necessitates silencing heretics:

> It posits a classic orthodoxy through which all of human experience is explained—and through which all speech must be filtered. Its version of original sin is the power of some identity groups over others. To overcome this sin, you need first to confess, i.e., "check your privilege," and subsequently live your life and order your thoughts in a way that keeps this sin at bay. The sin goes so deep into your psyche, especially if you are white or male or straight, that a profound conversion is required.
>
> Like the Puritanism once familiar in New England, intersectionality controls language and the very terms of discourse. It enforces manners. It has an idea of virtue—and is obsessed with upholding it. The saints are the most oppressed who nonetheless resist. The sinners are categorized in various ascending categories of demographic damnation, like something out of Dante. The only thing this religion lacks, of course, is salvation. Life is simply an interlocking drama of oppression and power and

resistance, ending only in death. It's Marx without the final total liberation.

It operates as a religion in one other critical dimension: If you happen to see the world in a different way, if you're a liberal or libertarian or even, gasp, a conservative, if you believe that a university is a place where any idea, however loathsome, can be debated and refuted, you are not just wrong, you are immoral. If you think that arguments and ideas can have a life independent of "white supremacy," you are complicit in evil. And you are not just complicit, your heresy is a direct threat to others, and therefore needs to be extinguished. You can't reason with heresy. You have to ban it. It will contaminate others' souls and wound them irreparably.[11]

Sullivan is one of the few voices in the establishment press willing to call attention to the toxic mob culture of the far left and its growing influence. *National Review*'s Kevin D. Williamson, for instance, barely lasted two weeks working at *The Atlantic* before left-wing mobs got him fired for his views on abortion. Williamson's left-wing detractors argued that his mere presence in the office could make his female colleagues unsafe.[12] On campus, things are even worse. Across the country, campus administrators have set up "bias reporting" hotlines for students to report their classmates for perceived thought-crimes, while left-wing academics admit to discriminating against conservative Ph.D. candidates.[13] When conservative speakers aren't routinely disinvited from speaking on college campuses, mobs of left-wing students have repeatedly used violence or intimidation to try to silence them.[14] In one famous incident in 2017, students at Middlebury College attacked author Charles Murray and a professor at the school, a liberal woman, who tried to help Murray escape the mob.[15]

As on college campuses, so too in public life when it is dominated by the far left. For example, I reported on how an independent, reformist candidate for city council in Seattle campaigning against "the ideologues" dominating city politics felt compelled to drop his candidacy after left-wing activists threatened his wife and children. As he said in a statement, "They've made vile, racist attacks against my wife, attempted to get her fired from Microsoft, and threatened sexual violence. They have even posted hateful messages to my eight-year-old son's school Facebook page. I know that as the race progresses, the activists will ratchet up their hate-machine and these attacks will intensify significantly."[16] When Trump supporters were attacked by violent protesters during the 2016 presidential campaign, the left often treated it as an open question as to whether it was the rioters or Trump's incendiary rhetoric that was at fault.[17] Of course, when you believe that speech that opposes your point of view is a form of violence, then you can justify real violence—or censorship—as a matter of self-defense.

Free speech, however, appeared to have a sanctuary on the Internet. Many of the popular political commentators on YouTube and Facebook had one thing in common: opposition to political correctness and the left-wing censorship it produced. When a video of Professor Jordan Peterson protesting mandatory "gender" speech codes went viral, he became a Facebook, YouTube, and Twitter sensation. Christina Hoff Sommers, a respected feminist scholar, and liberal-libertarian, garnered millions of views for her videos critiquing left-wing arguments on such topics as the alleged male-female wage gap and "toxic masculinity," and pointing to the feminist culture's "war on boys" in America's schools.[18] Ben Shapiro made viral internet videos his calling card, aiming them especially at college age viewers looking for thoughtful, alternative arguments to what they heard from professors, liberal politicians, and media talking heads. His success led to the creation of the popular website the

Daily Wire, which combines traditional online news commentary with podcasts from Shapiro and others.

Left-wing extremists have sometimes prevented Peterson, Shapiro, and Sommers from speaking on college campuses, but they haven't been able to stop them from speaking online (at least not yet). Nor could they stop the explosion of right-of-center media outlets online—like Breitbart, Daily Caller, Townhall, and many others—that filled a gaping hole in the media market.

■   ■   ■

The activist left was slow to realize the extent of the right's online success. Most progressives fawned over President Obama's use of Twitter and Facebook and assumed that their domination of establishment media would extend to online media, so they focused on trying to silence and discredit Fox News. Then the 2016 election happened.

Social media is one big reason that explains how candidate Donald Trump became President Donald Trump, as both the president and his 2020 campaign chair, Brad Parscale, have acknowledged. Parscale was the campaign's digital chief in the 2016 campaign. "I understood early that Facebook was how Donald Trump was going to win," he said in an October 2017 *60 Minutes* interview. "Twitter is how he talked to the people. Facebook was going to be how he won."[19] He added: "I think Donald Trump won [on his own], but I think Facebook was the method—it was the highway…his car drove on."

Hillary Clinton captured 96 percent of newspaper endorsements but lost the election.[20] If the result had been left up to the newsroom editors and cable TV anchors, Clinton would have won overwhelmingly. But it wasn't up to them, and she didn't, because of social media that helped candidate Donald Trump deliver his message—of economic nationalism, immigration enforcement, a stronger national defense, an America first foreign policy, the appointment of originalist judges, and support for pro-life policies and social conservatism—and reach voters disaffected from the mainstream media that preferred to dismiss all his policies as simply stupid and racist.

When Trump won the election, Democrats were furious because they had assumed they would win the White House in a landslide. Journalists were stunned because no one *they* knew had voted for Trump. And Silicon Valley was horrified, with many tech employees feeling guilty, wondering whether they should have done more to stop Trump on the platforms they controlled. Most important, left-wingers, both inside and outside of Silicon Valley, lost what little patience they had for conservative speech. They rationalized their intolerance by branding Trump and the nearly sixty-three million Americans who voted for him fascists, dupes of the Russians, or white supremacists. An honest response to the 2016 election from the left-liberal establishment would have been to realize that conservatives succeed online because they provide an alternative point of view that many Americans want to hear and that the mainstream media largely excludes. The media establishment could have done something to redress this imbalance and narrow its gap of trust with half of the country. Instead, they declared war on Trump and his supporters. The liberal mainstream news media became a propaganda arm of the Democratic National Committee, and the leftist mob has turned to the giants of Big Tech—and Big Government—and demanded that they silence voices on the right.

Jeffrey Rosen's prediction that a "mob with a dictator" would come to end free speech on the Internet has come to pass. The two major questions at this point are: 1) How far will this dangerous trend go? 2) What can be done to stop it?

CHAPTER TWO

Rigged

For better or worse, social media is the new public square. 68 percent of American adults use Facebook; 73 percent use You-Tube, and a quarter use Twitter. Those already high numbers are much higher for adults under fifty.[1] Two-thirds of American adults and roughly four-in-five adults under fifty use social media to consume their news.[2] Facebook plays such a pivotal role in Americans' daily lives and social interactions that CEO Mark Zuckerberg felt comfortable comparing it to religion in a June 2017 speech.[3] Three-quarters of Facebook users are on the site every day (not just Sunday),[4] and Twitter users have a disproportionate influence on the media because so many journalists are on Twitter.

Social media is all-encompassing and seemingly ever-present. Professional athletes stream Snapchat videos to their followers from locker rooms before games. Instagram is littered with "influencers" selling attire. Meeting romantic partners on social media or mobile apps is now commonplace. Presidential candidates livestream themselves on

Instagram doing housework and going to the dentist, and U.S. senators snipe at each other on Twitter—also the preferred social media platform of the President of the United States, who uses it for everything from conducting international diplomacy to ranting about his political enemies. It's mortifying, laughable, and awe-inspiring all at the same time.

The size and scale of social media companies exploded primarily because they presented themselves as open platforms—blank slates for people to use however they wanted. Google, Facebook, and Twitter all characterized their products as engines for social improvement. "We think of Twitter as the global town hall," said former Twitter CEO Dick Costolo. "We are the free speech wing of the free speech party."[5] Costolo was Twitter's chief executive from 2010 until 2015 and the immediate predecessor of current CEO Jack Dorsey. Twitter's general manager in the United Kingdom, Andy Yang, likewise described Twitter as the "free speech wing of the free speech party" in March 2012.[6] Google became a multibillion dollar company by offering a portal for free, unrestricted information to anyone with access to the Internet; famously, its original motto was "Don't be evil." An internal Facebook memo circulated in June 2016 stated that at Facebook, "we believe in connecting people so deeply that anything that allows us to connect more people more often is *de facto* good."[7] As we'll see, that's no longer the case at Facebook.

Americans have given these three major tech companies (and others) enormous power to select the information we read, share, and discuss with our neighbors and friends. We've gotten so accustomed to the role they play in our lives that we fail to even notice that Big Tech is sifting through the available information and narrowing—and prioritizing—our choices. Although Facebook, Google, and Twitter once touted themselves as bastions of democracy and free speech, they are now openly moving towards direct censorship and media manipulation. They say so themselves.

In March 2018, Google circulated an internal memo that instructed employees on the benefits of censorship. In the memo, which was titled "The Good Censor," Google conceded that while the Internet was "founded upon utopian principles of free speech," free speech is no longer en vogue.[8] The memo explained that "tech companies are adapting their stance towards censorship" in direct response to "the anxiety of users and governments." The memo conceded that "tech firms have gradually shifted away from unmediated free speech and towards censorship and moderation," but framed that shift as a positive development. One major way that tech companies are "stepping into the role of moderator" is by "significantly amping up the number of moderators they employ—in YouTube's case increasing the number of people on the lookout for inappropriate content to more than 10,000," the memo boasted.[9] It argued that censorship was necessary partly because of users "behaving badly," which required tech companies to oversee them. The most alarming part of the internal missive, however, was that it even spoke approvingly of foreign governments that were censoring online speech. Google framed the censorship as governments "taking steps to make online spaces safer, more regulated, and more similar to their offline laws. Protected from hate speech on the street? Now you are on the net too...."

Twitter has completely and publicly abandoned its brand as the "free speech wing of the free speech party." Jack Dorsey now claims that the whole "free speech wing" thing was one giant "joke." His company, once seemingly devoted to the free expression of its users, now says it is prioritizing making users feel safe from others' speech.[10]

Facebook, too, is openly rebranding itself as a benevolent censor. Here's what Facebook CEO Mark Zuckerberg told the Senate Commerce and Judiciary committees in April 2018 (emphasis added):

Overall, I would say that we're going through a broader philosophical shift in how we approach our responsibility as a company. For the first ten or twelve years of the company, I viewed our responsibility as primarily building tools that, if we could put those tools in people's hands, then that would empower people to do good things. What I think we've learned now across a number of issues—not just data privacy, but also fake news and foreign interference in elections—is that we need to take a more proactive role and a broader view of our responsibility. *It's not enough to just build tools. We need to make sure that they're used for good. And that means that we need to now take a more active view in policing the ecosystem and in watching and kind of looking out and making sure that all of the members in our community are using these tools in a way that's going to be good and healthy.*[11]

■   ■   ■

Three forces are driving Big Tech's online censorship. Two are external and related: market pressures and de-platforming campaigns by liberal activists and journalists. The third pressure is internal: Silicon Valley is staggeringly one-sided politically.

Profit margins and market pressures are crucial levers that left-wing ideologues use to pull tech giants and other corporations in the direction of censorship. Companies want to avoid controversy, and, in the era of outrage mobs, that means avoiding offending the left, which controls most of the cultural institutions in America. That's part of the reason why massive companies are embracing left-wing politics in advertising, like Gillette did with its "toxic masculinity" ad. Left-wing activists amplify those pressures with smear campaigns and boycotts intended to rattle advertisers and investors, forcing tech companies to take action. No company wants their name and "racist content" in the same sentence, regardless of whether the charge is true. If you convince corporate marketing agencies that advertising on Facebook is risky, you can be certain that Facebook will take some form of action to shed controversy and reassure investors.

The external pressures of left-wing activists are compounded by the internal pressures of the companies' employees, who want Big Tech to embrace censorship against non-progressive opinions as a moral and political necessity. The internal office cultures at Facebook, Google, and Twitter have always been overwhelmingly left-leaning, but the election of Donald Trump as president has made them far more radical. I told one Silicon Valley insider that I thought tech culture now resembled the left-wing activist culture on college campuses. He replied, "They're the exact same people."

Their political opinions are certainly monochromatic. Of the $8.1 million that tech industry workers donated to presidential candidates during the 2016 campaign, 95 percent of it went to Hillary Clinton. Among donations from the Silicon Valley area specifically, 99 *percent* went to Hillary Clinton.[12]

So maybe it's not surprising that Google, Facebook, and Twitter have all become vehicles for left-wing activism. The companies encourage employees to bring their "authentic selves" to work. One Silicon Valley executive told me, "We want people to…bring their entire perspective and all their values to work, and in the positive sense, that means getting rid of a huge distinction between my professional life and my personal life." For left-wing activists in Silicon Valley, their professional, personal, and political lives are all one. That's why Twitter launched an "intersectionality" initiative for its employees and Google gives millions to left-wing causes—to signal their allegiance to the tribe and placate its members. As a lawsuit by former Google employee James Damore made clear, conservatives have to hide their opinions and remain silent or face retribution at the high tech giant, but support for the violent, extremist ideology of Antifa can be freely expressed.[13]

What the Numbers Show

In 2017, the nonprofit Lincoln Network conducted a survey of tech workers in Silicon Valley, including those employed at Google, Facebook, Apple, Amazon, and Microsoft. The political leanings of those surveyed were more politically diverse than Silicon Valley's overall population: 29 percent were liberal; 24 percent were libertarian; 22 percent were conservative; and 16 percent were moderate. But on one thing they agreed. 75 percent of the liberals and 70 percent of the conservatives characterized their workplace as either "liberal" or "very liberal" and fewer than 2 percent of the survey-takers said their places of work were conservative.[14]

Even some of the liberal respondents thought that left-wing intolerance had gone too far. One liberal tech worker said, "I witnessed repeated calls from managers and non-managers alike for people to be fired for the political views they expressed." Another liberal employee said, "There are people who are looking for a reason to be offended, and any sort of disagreement would make them wonder if I'm a secret Trump supporter. The idea of 'I agree with you 90 percent' is not enough."

One self-identified libertarian said, "I have lost multiple talented colleagues who resigned rather than continue in the face of an increasingly extreme, narrow-minded, and regressive environment here at Google. It's terrifying here. A real horror show. Every day could be my last."

89 percent of respondents who identified as "very conservative" said they didn't feel comfortable expressing their opinions at work. "It's a postmodern, secularist Silicon Valley viewpoint. Highly liberal. It's motivated by changing the world masquerading as intellectualism," said one conservative tech employee.

A libertarian said that "there were many groups devoted to identity politics" in his company, and every one of them was leftist. "If you're not part of the liberal Democrat crowd, you're an outsider. Talks are often politicized, whether overtly or not. The entire executive team leans in a certain direction, and you don't want to be the odd one out for fear of being ostracized.... Nobody who didn't fit the company's mold talked about their political views. The company was very homogenous in that sense."

One conservative employee said, "There is overwhelming internal support for leftist political candidates, policies, and ideas, and they are frequently expressed.... There are zero to very few senior people who dare to speak up or represent an alternative (more conservative) point of view in company debates or policy decisions."

A libertarian employee said. "At times when I have had a difference of opinion, I have been retaliated against, bullied, verbally intimidated...." A conservative added, "It is unsafe to have any discussions in Silicon Valley that do not subscribe to its tyrannical groupthink. I believe they're already trying to push me out of the industry."

A libertarian employee alleged that at Apple there is "a concerted purge of conservative employees."

Another libertarian said: "There are certain things you *can't* talk about...without serious risk to your career."

This groupthink affects everything that Big Tech does, every decision it makes, every program it releases. As a former Google engineer noted, despite the company's protestations that its algorithms are programmed for the interests of everyone, Google's algorithms reflect the assumptions and biases of their creators.[15]

■   ■   ■

The Censorship You See—and the Censorship You Don't

The discussion about tech platforms and political bias often (and understandably) centers on what is or isn't allowed on Google, YouTube, Facebook, and Twitter—but the other half of the picture is what is and isn't *prioritized* on a platform.

Broadly speaking, tech companies censor users and content in two ways. The first, which we'll call "hard censorship," is pretty straightforward: deleting content or suspending users. The second method, which we'll call "soft censorship," involves tech companies making content harder to find. Hard censorship is tearing down a roadside billboard; soft censorship is making the billboard difficult to see by erecting other billboards in front of it.

Soft censorship by tech companies can be just as effective as hard censorship. Studies show that people rarely click past the first page of Google or YouTube results. Even fewer click past the second or third page. So, pushing a link off the first page (or two or three) of Google is nearly the same as removing it from Google results altogether. The same is true with your Facebook and Twitter feeds: companies don't have to delete content to make sure you don't see it.

■   ■   ■

Since 2016, every major tech company—including Facebook, Google, YouTube, and Twitter—has been busy re-tooling algorithms or news feeds or monetization standards in ways that benefit liberals and sideline conservatives. Big Tech also partners with left-wing groups like the Southern Poverty Law Center (SPLC) to "flag" alleg-edly problematic content. The SPLC falsely labels individual conser-vatives as "extremists" and conservative organizations as "hate groups," and then promotes more restrictive content policies against alleged "hate speech."[16] To give you some idea of the SPLC's stan-dards, it once accused Dr. Ben Carson of being an "extremist" for stating his belief that marriage is between a man and a woman.[17] Immersed in scandals of its own,[18] the SPLC has been widely discred-ited.[19] But it still works closely with Google engineers who design the digital tools and algorithms to police hate speech on YouTube as part of Google's "Trusted Flaggers" program.[20] Google kept its collabora-tion with the SPLC a secret, hidden behind a confidentiality agree-ment, and the SPLC only admitted the partnership after I broke the story.[21] All of these partnerships are occurring while the SPLC pub-licly keeps pressure on Facebook, Google, and Twitter, calling for them to do more to combat "hate speech" on their platforms, which invariably means giving the SPLC more power in their private deal-ings with the companies.

The SPLC led five other left-wing groups in forming a coalition called "Change the Terms" that aims to pressure all major technol-ogy service providers into setting speech codes that govern what their clients say both on *and off* their platforms. The coalition demands that each company agree to implement a specific set of policies already drafted by the activists. Among the required changes: empowering third-party organizations (like, say, the SPLC) to flag "hateful" actors. The activists' targets aren't limited to Facebook, Google, and Twitter (although those companies are certainly on the list) but also include credit card companies and crowdfunding sites. Once a company caves to the pressure and agrees to adopt the left-wing contract, it has essentially deputized the SPLC to decide who can stay on its platform or use its services and who must leave. (After all, under this arrangement, it is the SPLC who defines who is an "extremist.") Once the contract is official, the activists immediately shift gears to identifying the users or customers the company is now required to ban from its platform. As we'll see, the left-wingers' plan for weaponizing tech platforms bears resemblance to the "Social Credit Score" system adopted by the Chinese government. Only instead of the government monitoring your private behavior and limiting your access to society as a result, it's a collective of left-wing advocacy groups partnered with multinational corporations. Activists are working to harness the power of Big Tech and commerce to implement ideas that are similar in principle to those practiced by Communist China, and there is no law that can stop them; First Amendment rights do not protect you from private organizations' limitations on speech. It's a devious strategy, and it's working.

Media Matters is a left-wing political group devoted to silencing conservative viewpoints in the media. For much of its history, it focused on attacking Fox News, but in recent years it has targeted conservative voices online as well. Media Matters presented a forty-four-page memo to liberal donors at a January 2017 summit that bragged about its plans to work with Facebook and Google to destroy non-liberal media outlets.[22] The memo argued that enlisting Big Tech in the left-wing campaign to destroy conservative media is essential if liberals hope to defeat Donald Trump in 2020. Media Matters promised to accomplish exactly that. "Key right-wing targets will see their influence diminished as a result of our work," the left-wing group promised. The leftists don't need to banish every conservative from social media, they only need to dominate social media the way they dominate the mainstream media. They're okay with discussion that takes place within boundaries they set (as on MSNBC), and as long they win the elections that matter to them (like the White House). Since November 8,

2016, they have shifted the digital landscape against conservative voices. By November 3, 2020, they will have transformed (or rigged) social media in ways that will have far-reaching implications for America.

CHAPTER THREE

Facebook

Facebook's influence over the American population is astounding: seven in ten Americans use Facebook, and three-quarters of those users say they're on Facebook every single day, an early 2019 Pew Research Center study found.[1] A September 2018 Pew study found that 43 percent of Americans obtain news primarily through Facebook, leading the research institute to conclude that Facebook "is still far and away the site Americans most commonly use for news."[2]

Facebook wields enormous power over its users and has no qualms about exercising it. The tech giant collaborated with academics from Cornell and the University of California San Francisco to conduct experiments on the effects that tweaks to its News Feed algorithm had on users' emotional states. The kicker: Facebook used its customers as guinea pigs in the experiment without their knowledge.[3] In the experiment, which involved a jaw-dropping 689,000 users, Facebook manipulated individuals' newsfeeds by increasing the share of positive material presented to some users and increasing the share of negative material presented to others. The results of the experiment revealed that Facebook could influence an individual user's own posts in a positive or negative direction by skewing the information the user was exposed to on his or her news feed.[4] In other words, Facebook tested its societal influence by tampering with the emotional states of private citizens without their consent. Facebook did so without remorse.

When Facebook's malfeasance was uncovered, the company's second-in-command, Sheryl Sandberg, was unapologetic in the face of the scandal.[5] "This was part of ongoing research companies do to test different products, and that was what it was; it was poorly communicated. And for that communication we apologize. We never meant to upset you," she told the *Wall Street Journal*.[6] Note: Sandberg's statement was not an apology for treating other human beings—many of whom doubtlessly used the platform for purposes like sharing pictures of their grandchildren or reconnecting with high school classmates—like guinea pigs in a laboratory. Sandberg's only apology was for not doing a better job selling the initiative to the public. Facebook's willingness to manipulate its users' emotions—and its willingness to study the best way to do so—is important to keep in mind as the company pledges to manipulate America out of political polarization. Facebook has a history of quietly exerting its power to influence political opinions in America without its users' knowledge. When the Black Lives Matter movement was still in its nascent stage, for example, the Facebook employees who oversaw the company's "trending topics" section received an order: push Black Lives Matter into trending topics.[7] Whatever you think about Black Lives Matter, Facebook wasn't reacting to its audience—it was manipulating its audience. The manipulation was made public only after former employees blew the whistle on Facebook's conduct.[8]

They also reported that the Black Lives Matter episode was not an isolated incident, and that conservative news and commentators were consistently downplayed.[9] Facebook later dropped its trending topics function in favor of its retooled NewsFeed, which is easier for the company to manipulate without public knowledge.

Facebook's Leftists

Facebook is an institutionally left-wing organization. Sources describe a workplace where communists and marxists are more welcome than conservatives and Republicans. Facebook's internal operations and communications are conducted on a closed version of the site, called Facebook Workplace. The internal platform is basically like the Facebook used by members of the public, but its visibility is limited to the roughly 30,000 employees who work at the company. Facebook employees often interact on the internal platform with coworkers they don't know or have never actually met. Employees who dissent from progressive dogma are often targeted on the platform, and subjected to vicious personal attacks from the left-wing mob, so most dissenters stay quiet. As Facebook senior engineer Brian Amerige wrote, in an internal memo criticizing the political intolerance within the company, "We claim to welcome all perspectives, but are quick to attack—often in mobs—anyone who presents a view that appears to be in opposition to left-leaning ideology."[10]

Amerige launched a group called FB'ers for Political Diversity dedicated to open debate within the company. But at Facebook, political diversity is the wrong kind of diversity. In internal message boards and at town halls, employees demanded to know why Facebook was allowing "hate speech" to take place within the company. Amerige isn't a Republican or a social conservative. He's a self-described objectivist, closer to a libertarian than anything else. But as far as most Facebook employees were concerned, Amerige was a bigot, a racist, a sexist, a transphobe, and a litany of other horrible things. Amerige resigned from Facebook in October 2018, explaining in another memo that he was "burnt out on Facebook, our strategy, and our culture." Here's an excerpt:

> Strategically, we've taken a stance on how to balance offensive and hateful speech with free expression. We've accepted the inevitability of government regulation. And we've refused to defend ourselves in the press. Our policy strategy is pragmatism—not clear, implementable long-term principles—and our PR strategy is appeasement—not morally earned pride and self-defense.
>
> Culturally, it's difficult to have meaningful conversations about any of this because we're a political monoculture, and these are political issues. And while we've made some progress in FB'ers for Political Diversity (which is approaching 750 members now), and while I'm pleased to say that senior company leadership does take this seriously (as you will hopefully soon see), we have a very long way to go.
>
> To that end, while I remain as in love as ever with our mission and my colleagues' nearly-always good intentions, I disagree too strongly with where we're heading on these issues to watch what happens next. These issues hang over my head each morning, and I don't want to spend all of my time fighting about them.[11]

■   ■   ■

Facebook employees were all-in on team Hillary during the 2016 general election, even trying to delete Trump's campaign posts for alleged "hate speech," until Zuckerberg overruled them.[12] Zuckerberg, still hurting from the trending topics scandal, insisted that it wasn't

Facebook's role to swing elections, though that argument carried less weight with left-wing employees after Trump's surprise victory, and Zuckerberg was quick to announce that Facebook would be improving its monitoring of "fake news" on the site.

One Facebook employee who dissented from the anti-Trump culture put up signs stating "Trump supporters welcome here." Signs are welcome at the Facebook campus and are considered part of the culture, but these signs were torn down almost as rapidly as he could post them. Internal company chats lit up with anger over the incident—not because a colleague was being silenced, but because that colleague had dared to assert that Trump supporters could possibly be welcome at Facebook.

Wealth and status in Silicon Valley aren't enough to save you from the outrage mobs, which spare no heretic. Oculus VR co-founder Palmer Luckey, whose company Facebook had acquired two years before in a multi-billion-dollar deal, found himself on the ropes at the company after he donated $10,000 to a political action committee opposing Clinton's candidacy. In both internal message boards and at company town halls, Facebook employees demanded that Luckey be fired.[13] "Multiple women have literally teared up in front of me in the last few days," engineering director Srinivas Narayanan claimed in an internal post.[14] Luckey later posted an apology that clarified that he would vote for Libertarian Party candidate Gary Johnson, rather than Trump, in the 2016 election. Facebook fired him in March 2017, two months after Trump took office. Zuckerberg later testified under oath that Luckey's firing was unrelated to politics, but the *Wall Street Journal* blew up that lie in a November 2018 article titled: "Political Clash Led to Firing of Top Facebook Executive." Among the details that came out: Mark Zuckerberg himself had drafted the apology Luckey later posted under his own name.[15]

Facebook executives publicly supported Clinton throughout her campaign. They were among her biggest and most enthusiastic supporters. Luckey's sin was not that he expressed political opinions, it was that he expressed the wrong ones. He defied the left-wing mobs (or at least tried to), and he paid the price.

Facebook vs. Kavanaugh

As it was elsewhere in Silicon Valley, Trump's election was a punch to the gut for Facebook employees who had counted on Hillary Clinton coasting to victory. Facebook vice president Julie Zhuo was still so upset the morning after the election that she became physically ill. She later broke down in tears. "This election meant so much to so many people. It felt like the values of tolerance, equality, respect, and competence lost out. My heart breaks for Hillary and for Obama," she wrote on Facebook, in response to Trump's election.[16] Zhuo pledged to "create better tools" at Facebook "to encourage understanding and empathy between people of different beliefs." Zhuo's coworkers were just as shocked. "I just didn't think this would be the outcome," another Facebook vice president, Carolyn Everson, reflected afterwards. She vowed to raise her children as "global citizens."[17]

But if Facebook's employees were shocked by Trump's victory, they were prepared for political war when the president nominated judge Brett Kavanaugh to fill the Supreme Court seat of retiring Justice Anthony Kennedy. And they were in for another shock when Facebook vice president Joel Kaplan, a rare Republican at Facebook, and a friend of Kavanaugh's, sat behind the judge during his testimony: a quiet show of support for his friend during the most difficult moments of his life. Kaplan supported Kavanaugh in his personal capacity only. He wasn't representing Facebook, just as Facebook chief operating officer Sheryl Sandberg wasn't representing the company when she personally endorsed Hillary Clinton for president in 2016. There was nothing wrong with Kaplan's actions, but Facebook employees bubbled with rage anyway. Internal message boards logged hundreds of comments from leftist Facebook employees incensed at Kaplan's support for his friend. One program manager called Kaplan's decision to sit behind Kavanaugh "a protest against our culture, and a slap in the face to his fellow employees"[18]—exposing what the whole controversy was really about: conformance to the left-wing culture. Facebook CEO Mark Zuckerberg pointed out that Kaplan had violated no company rules, but that did not appease the left-wing mob at Facebook. At a company town hall, an executive was shouted down when he tried to answer questions about Kaplan and Kavanaugh; the questioner wanted answers from Mark Zuckerberg himself. Zuckerberg obliged, but it still didn't pacify the mob; they wanted Kaplan fired.

For her part, Sheryl Sandberg was more than willing to throw Kaplan under the bus. "As a woman and someone who cares so deeply about how women are treated, the Kavanaugh issue is deeply upsetting to me. I've talked to Joel about why I think it was a mistake for him to attend given his role in the company," she wrote in an internal post. "We support people's right to do what they want in their personal time but this was by no means a straightforward case." Sandberg, once a staffer in the Clinton administration, had supported Hillary Clinton's presidential campaign both privately and publicly, and shared personally commissioned research with it.[19] Kaplan's mild show of support for his friend, Kavanaugh, however, was a bridge too far for Sandberg. Kaplan isn't exactly a hard right-winger, either: like Kavanaugh, he's an establishment Republican of the Jeb Bush variety. But the left didn't care. He was still the enemy.

Silicon Valley melted down when Kavanaugh was confirmed. "You are finished, GOP. You polished the final nail in your own coffins. FUCK. YOU. ALL. TO. HELL," Google lead designer David Hogue wrote on Twitter when Kavanagh's confirmation appeared certain. "I hope the last images burned into your slimy, evil retinas are millions of women clapping and celebrating as your souls descend into the flames." A Facebook content manager tweeted, "51 people have announced their support for Kavanaugh. Let's hold them ALL accountable. (Some are even up for election next month!)"[20]

Facebook employees seethed, and soon leaks to the media pointed to Kaplan as a roadblock to Facebook's becoming more progressive. "Mr. Kaplan is Facebook's longtime global policy chief, but his remit has expanded considerably in the last two years. He has often been the decisive word internally on hot-button political issues and has wielded his influence to postpone or kill projects that risk upsetting conservatives," the *Wall Street Journal* reported in December 2018. "Many current and former Facebook insiders argue that the company's desire to avoid criticism from conservatives prevents it from fully tackling broader issues on the platform," the *Journal*'s report added. A sizable segment of Facebook employees believes that rules are only good if they lead to left-wing outcomes. If they feel they can attack a Facebook vice president and try to get him fired because they don't like his political friends, imagine how they plan to monitor content on the site.

The Bait-and-Switch

Big tech companies have shifted the way they talk about their roles as national speech monitors. Their early efforts were ostensibly focused on fighting harassment, violent threats, and fake news sites like "Patriot News Agency."[21] Four days after Trump's election, Facebook CEO Mark Zuckerberg announced that the company would work to combat "fake news" and "hoaxes." He also sounded a note of caution, stressing the need for Facebook to "be extremely cautious about becoming arbiters of truth ourselves."[22] Nevertheless, Facebook announced on December 15, 2016, that it was partnering with five outside fact-checkers who would soon be the arbiters of truth on Facebook: PolitiFact, ABC News, FactCheck.org, the AP, and Snopes.[23] All these organizations lean to the left, but Snopes has the most egregious track record, consistently racking up errors and spreading misinformation itself. Facebook eventually added the anti-Trump conservative magazine the *Weekly Standard* to the program. But the *Standard* folded in December 2018, leaving Facebook's fact-checkers once again exclusively left-leaning until Facebook added the Daily Caller's fact-checking arm to the program, thus restoring the five-to-one liberal-conservative "balance."

As fake news sites (which were largely insignificant in the first place[24]) have disappeared and liberal activists have pushed for even more censorship, tech companies have changed their rationale for speech policing. In November 2018, Zuckerberg touted Facebook's "broader social responsibility to help bring people closer together— against polarization and extremism. The past two years have shown that without sufficient safeguards, people will misuse these tools to interfere in elections, spread misinformation, and incite violence." His post was titled "A Blueprint for Content Governance and Enforcement"[25] and noted that Facebook has "a responsibility to keep people safe on our services—whether from terrorism, bullying, or other threats."

Zuckerberg claimed, "One of the biggest issues social networks face is that, when left unchecked, people will engage disproportionately with more sensationalist and provocative content. This is not a new phenomenon. It is widespread on cable news today and has been a staple of tabloids for more than a century. At scale it can undermine the quality of public discourse and lead to polarization. This is a basic incentive problem that we can address by penalizing borderline content so it gets less distribution and engagement. By making the distribution curve look like the graph below where distribution declines as content gets more sensational, people are disincentivized from creating provocative content that is as close to the line as possible." He added that the "category we're most focused on is click-bait and misinformation."

Zuckerberg's manifesto was noteworthy for a couple of reasons. First, Zuckerberg publicly conceded that Facebook intended to manipulate its users, (allegedly away from political polarization). Second, it was entirely disingenuous about eliminating "clickbait." Check out the following headlines posted to Facebook and guess where they came from:

- "A dad longed to spend Christmas with his flight attendant daughter. He found a clever way."
- "You really, really want to go to the gym but still avoid it. New research may explain why."
- "The 10 weirdest celebrity apologies of 2018, from a cemetery selfie to a very awkward tweet."
- "The game of their lives was 25 years ago. They're still replaying it in their minds."

Those are clickbait headlines. In fact, they're great clickbait headlines. And they're all courtesy of the *Washington Post*, which regularly and shamelessly publishes clickbait on Facebook, and continues to do so because Facebook has no intention of punishing the *Washington Post*. When Zuckerberg says clickbait what he really means is conservative-inspired headlines.

Zuckerberg is equally disingenuous when he talks about disincentivizing people from creating "provocative content." Provocative content drives the media. CNN's Jim Acosta has made a career out of being provocative as a White House reporter. Speculating about whether the president has been a Russian agent for decades, as *New*

York Magazine columnist Jonathan Chait did, is provocative.[26] It's provocative to run articles promoting polyamory, as the *New York Times* and other liberal media outlets have done.[27] When Facebook talks about punishing provocative voices on its platform, are those the voices it intends to punish? Not a chance.

When Facebook executives talk about punishing provocative content, they are referring to politically incorrect conservative voices—everything from pro-life content to videos of Ben Shapiro or Jordan Peterson—with which they passionately disagree. Reporting on scandals at Planned Parenthood is provocative, in the eyes of the activist left. So is reporting on Facebook and Google's left-wing biases. Reporting on friendships between Democratic members of Congress and Nation of Islam leader Louis Farrakhan—a notorious antisemite—is provocative. As Facebook dials up its suppression on provocative content and clickbait, it won't be outlets like the *Washington Post* that bear the brunt of that suppression, no matter how many clickbait headlines they run.

Facebook once preached that making people more connected was its only goal, but the tech giant is now making "provocative" groups harder to find. "This is especially important to address because while social networks in general expose people to more diverse views, and while groups in general encourage inclusion and acceptance, divisive groups and pages can still fuel polarization," Zuckerberg explained in November 2018.[28]

Stating facts like "men can't become women" or "abortion ends a human life" is provocative in liberal circles. So is believing that marriage is a sacrament between a man and woman, as the Catholic Church teaches. You can expect Silicon Valley to treat these ideas as not only provocative, but scandalous.

Facebook's insistence on keeping its processes a secret does not inspire confidence. Zuckerberg is entirely unconcerned about the principles of free speech and freedom of association on the platform and entirely concerned about protecting the company's image. That's both my impression and the impression of sources who have spoken with him repeatedly about the issue. By the time he released his manifesto in November 2018, Facebook had already laid the groundwork to vastly overhaul its platform to benefit the liberal establishment.

Facebook NewsFeed

In January 2018, Zuckerberg announced two key changes to Facebook's newsfeed algorithm that together would boost a "trusted" minority of news outlets while suppressing their competitors. First, Facebook would slash news articles' share of the newsfeed from 5 percent to 4 percent in the coming months. Second, Facebook would boost certain "trusted" news outlets and suppress other sources that it determined less trustworthy. At the time, Facebook said that trustworthiness would be determined by a simple two-question poll: whether a user had heard of a publication, and whether they trusted it. That turned out not to be the case.

While speaking at a tech conference in February 2018, Facebook executive Campbell Brown indicated that Facebook would boost "quality" news sources, even if they didn't have widespread name recognition (and thus polled poorly in Facebook's two-question poll). "So much of the best journalism today is being done by smaller, more niche, more focused journalists who aren't gonna have the brand recognition," Brown said. "To me, this is the future of journalism. This is where the experts are gonna be." Brown, herself a former NBC and CNN anchor, said Facebook was now going to have a "point of view" towards the news. In other words, the poll was just a cover for boosting the outlets Facebook wanted to boost, whether they polled well or not. "This is us changing our relationship with publishers and emphasizing something that Facebook has never done before: It's having a point of view, and it's leaning into quality news," Brown said of the newsfeed changes. She added that Facebook is "taking a step to try to define what quality news looks like and give that a boost."[29]

Not surprisingly, Facebook's algorithm changes overwhelmingly benefited establishment liberal media outlets. In April 2018, News-Whip—one of the most respected, non-partisan, social media analytics companies—reported: "The changes could be divided into two fairly distinct camps: engagement boosts for mainstream news outlets such as CNN and NBC, and declines for smaller, politically-focused sites and entertainment publishers."[30] NewsWhip noted that "of the top ten most engaged sites in March [2018], eight were legacy news outlets. Looking at individual sites, it's clear that some names, namely CNN, the *New York Times*, *The Guardian*, BBC News, and the *Washington Post*, all posted dramatic increases in their interaction counts.... Increases of this magnitude had not been seen in a long time." And who were the losers? The digital companies giving the establishment media a run for their money. "If large mainstream news sites with TV or print arms were the big winners in terms of engagement and attention last month, their most prominent digital rivals of the last few years were the losers. In particular, smaller political news sites and entertainment or viral outlets saw their engagement diminish."

The algorithm changes disproportionately harmed right-of-center publishers, tech website The Outline concluded in a lengthy report earlier in March 2018. The Outline's analysis found that "conservative and right-wing publishers (such as Breitbart, Fox News, and Gateway Pundit) were hit the hardest in the weeks following the announcement, with Facebook engagement totals for February dropping as much as 55 percent for some, while the engagement numbers of most predominantly liberal publishers remained unaffected."[31] Conservative website

Western Journalism reached the same conclusion in its own analysis published the same month: conservative websites saw a significant drop in traffic from Facebook following the algorithm change, while comparable liberal sources saw a slight increase.[32] Facebook's series of post-election changes damaged many media outlets on the right, and destroyed two of them.

Independent Journal Review, or IJR, was a major player in the conservative media world in 2016 and 2017. It was the first outlet to report that Trump had picked Neil Gorsuch to serve on the Supreme Court. It got another major scoop with exclusive access to Secretary of State Rex Tillerson on his first trip to Asia. In a March 2017 piece for *Business Insider*, Oliver Darcy, now at CNN, described IJR as a "powerhouse."[33] That was then. Now, IJR is essentially a non-player in the media world. Facebook's algorithm changes to start off 2018 neutered IJR's traffic, leaving the outlet a skeleton of what it once was.[34] Before February 2018 was over, the company cleaned house with mass layoffs.[35]

News and culture website Rare went from being a popular conservative media outlet, to being gutted and sold after Facebook's algorithm changes. The website's traffic fluctuated in 2017, in part because Facebook's newly hired content monitors erroneously classified Rare as an "ad farm" without informing the site. It was only when Rare reached out to Facebook in October 2017 that the site was able to find out what the hell was going on with its traffic. By November 2017, the error had been corrected and Rare's traffic returned, former Rare writer Matt Naham recounted.[36] "Then January 2018 happened." Rare's traffic plummeted once again, except this time it stayed there. Rare informed staffers on March 1, 2018, that they would all be unemployed by the end of the month.[37] But Facebook was just getting started.

Three months later, in May 2018, Zuckerberg elaborated on how the boosting and suppression of certain media outlets was—and is—taking place: "We put [that data] into the system, and it is acting as a boost or a suppression, and we're going to dial up the intensity of that over time," he told BuzzFeed. "We feel like we have a responsibility to further [break] down polarization and find common ground."[38] It's important to note that when Facebook executives talk about "breaking down political polarization," they're talking about manipulating their algorithms to sway people's political perspectives. And when they talk about politically polarized Americans, they aren't talking about liberals. The hivemind in Facebook doesn't see left-wingers as polarized—after all, the vast majority of their employees find common ground in left-wing politics. They see the people who reject left-wing politics as polarized and in need of correction. That's who they believe were the problem in 2016, and that's who they're trying to change. Thus, "ending polarization" does not mean moving each side slightly in the other's direction; it means moving everyone on the right to the left. If not for pushback from Kaplan, Facebook would already have implemented an algorithm change inserting opposing views into certain users' feeds.[39] Unsurprisingly, the proposed plan would have overwhelmingly targeted conservative users.[40] The program was a blatant attempt by Facebook to ram CNN and HuffPost articles down the throats of people who don't want to read them. When Facebook talks about breaking down "polarization," this is what the company means: prescribing liberal thoughts to cure conservatives of their conservatism.

It also means the perpetuation of the establishment media monoculture. Facebook in 2019 began rolling out an entirely new section of the site—Facebook News—for a handpicked set of media outlets. Some of them would be paid — big league. The *Wall Street Journal* reported in August 2019 that Facebook had proposed million-dollar partnerships to establishment media companies.[41] "The outlets pitched by Facebook on its news tab included Walt Disney Co.'s ABC

News, *Wall Street Journal* parent Dow Jones, the *Washington Post,* and Bloomberg," the *Journal* reported. Campbell Brown, the CNN anchor–turned Big Tech executive, officially introduced Facebook News to the public on October 25, 2019. At the top of the "key features" section: "Today's Stories" which would be "chosen by a team of journalists"—working for Facebook—"to catch you up on the news throughout the day." That is: the news you see on Facebook would now be hand-selected by Facebook.

The new feature effectively created three tiers of media outlets on Facebook. The top tier—as designated by Facebook's left-wing workforce—not only received access to the news tab and first choice for the "Today's Stories" section, they also received access to Facebook's wallet. The second tier would have access to the new feature—but they wouldn't be paid for it. And the third tier was shut out altogether. Facebook is paying some of the favored outlets as much as $3 million per year.[42] The company noted that Breitbart News was among the outlets whose articles would be included in Facebook News, though not directly paid for it like Facebook's favorites would be. Establishment journalists seethed that Breitbart made it into the second tier, instead of being barred from Facebook News through and through.

"Experts assail: If Breitbart is 'high quality' news, what's low?" wrote CNN's Oliver Darcy, noting that he "reached out to some experts in the journalism field to ask them what they thought of Facebook's decision. None were supportive."[43] The three "experts" Darcy cited were: a left-wing Columbia University professor, a *Washington Post* blogger and MSNBC contributor Charlie Sykes. The editor in chief of The Daily Beast, a liberal website, accused Facebook of "embracing a political ideology" by allowing Breitbart into the second tier.[44] Charlie Warzel, a liberal columnist at the *New York Times*, devoted an entire column to raking Facebook over the coals for Breitbart's inclusion.[45]

The left-wing rage at Facebook, if anything, was helpful to the company. Left-wingers insisting Facebook's bias didn't go far enough distracted from just how far the company had gone. Facebook is no longer a free and open platform — it's a platform explicitly designed to give a leg up to specific outlets. A sliver of the right-of-center media world made the cut, in order to present a cheap claim to fairness. They let Facebook pretend as if it's at all politically neutral. It's not permanent safety, either. They're at Facebook's mercy—and Facebook will face greater and greater pressure from the left to kick right-of-center outlets further down the ladder.

It's worth noting the way in which Facebook has overhauled its platform: gradually. Since the 2016 election, the play for Silicon Valley has been to slow-walk content changes that have massive political implications, while insisting with a straight face that there are no political implications to those changes. There's a tremendous upside to handling the process that way: changes receive the most attention when they're announced, allowing Facebook to dismiss critics as conspiracy theorists—after all, the platform looks largely the same as the day before. Then, as suspicion and scrutiny fade, Facebook can slowly but surely "dial up" the manipulation. Step by step, in reaction to one election and in preparation for another, Facebook will have dramatically overhauled how news is consumed on its platform, and particularly *which* news outlets most people see: the outlets that favor the establishment left.

"Facebook is kind of like the world's newsstand. Imagine if one company owned all the newsstands in America and decided that some newspapers couldn't be available in any stand in America, I think people would have a huge speech problem with that, and that's essentially what's going on now," is how reporter Allum Bokhari described Facebook's overhaul of its platform to me.

Facebook would punish content that doesn't break the rules (but that Facebook monitors don't like), pay and promote liberal publishers through Facebook News, and, most of all, single-out conservatives for special negative treatment.

Any time Facebook makes a change to its content policies, conservative voices end up worse off for it. It's not a coincidence that Facebook's "mistakes" always target the liberal establishment's opponents. Consider a few examples:

Franklin Graham

Facebook suspended the Reverend Franklin Graham in December 2018 for a two-year-old post about transgender bathrooms. The 2016 post advocated for a proposed North Carolina law requiring persons, including people who identify as transgender, to use the bathroom of their biological sex. Graham argued the law would "prevent men from being able to use women's restrooms and locker rooms." He thought that was a common-sense good thing to do. But it was too much for one of Facebook's content monitors, who reviewed the post after someone—it's unclear who—flagged the two-year-old Facebook post for hate speech. Facebook's content reviewer agreed, ruling that the post was in violation of Facebook's rules against "dehumanizing language."[46] After a backlash from conservative users, Facebook issued an apology to Graham and said the suspension was an error.[47] "Facebook is censoring free speech," Graham reflected afterwards. "They're making and changing the rules. Truth is truth. God made the rules and His Word is truth. The free exchange of ideas is part of our country's DNA."[48]

"Men Can't Be Women"

Facebook suspended right-wing British writer Raheem Kassam in May 2019 for challenging the left-wing position on transgender issues. Kassam's original post, from 2008, said "men can't be women."[49] He re-shared the post eleven years later in 2019, adding: "How did I know all this trans shit was coming, eleven years ago?" Facebook suspended him for a week. "This is because you've previously posted something that didn't follow our Community Standard," Facebook informed him. "This post goes against our standards on hate speech, so no one else can see it."[50]

#BuildThatWall

Facebook flagged a post honoring slain California police officer Ronil Singh.[51] The post noted that Singh, a legal immigrant, was murdered in the line of duty by an illegal immigrant. "This is precisely why we need to #buildthatwall," the post said. Facebook deleted the post until the Daily Caller News Foundation inquired about its deletion.[52]

A Rabbi Walks onto a Train with Anti-Semites

Big Tech's rigid adherence to progressive ideology explains why the censorship and suppression invariably skews against certain groups and in favor of others. New York Rabbi Avram Mlotek learned this lesson firsthand. Just days after an antisemite murdered eleven people at a Pittsburgh synagogue, Mlotek was riding the train home when he found himself on the receiving end of vicious antisemitism. He recounted the frightening experience in a lengthy Facebook post:

> "You a Jew, man?" I was asked on a crowded uptown B train headed home. "I am, brother," I replied. "You a real Jew, man?" he pressed. "I try," I answered. "Blacks are Jews, man," he said. "Yes, Jews come in all colors, brother,"

I said. "Nah, I'm a real Jew," he said, "You're an impostor." I stopped engaging at this point while this man told me repeatedly that Israel was not mine, that I was a fraud, and that Jews are responsible for the mess we find ourselves in today in the city of New York and all over the world. He then lifted up a picture of Louis Farrakhan and asked, "You know who this is?" I didn't answer. He kept asking and asked louder. "Yes," I said, "that's an anti-semite." "No," he said, "that's a real Jew. You're a fu*king fake." At this point another man on the subway said, "He ain't gonna take your bait." The first man then said, "Yeah, brother. Black power." The second man about me, "He a photocopy" and lifted up his fist in the Black power symbol. The first man went on: "And a bunch of them are gays. Fu*king faggots. You gonna get off this subway stop, man?" "I'm going to go home to my wife and kids," I said. "Yeah, you a cocks*cker," he said. "Have a blessed night," I said as I got off the train. On a crowded subway home, no one besides a second man who seemingly held similar ideologies said anything.

Rabbi Mlotek's post was a horrifying, eye-opening example of anti-Semitism in America. Yet Facebook deleted it for allegedly violating "community standards." Since antisemitism in New York comes largely from the far left,[53] one has to wonder what those "community standards are. Facebook didn't restore the post until Aaron Bandler, a reporter with the *Jewish Journal*, asked about the removal. After Bandler's inquiry, the social media company restored the post, which it said was "mistakenly" deleted. The *New York Times*, the *Washington Post*, the *Wall Street Journal*, HuffPost, and BuzzFeed combined to write a grand total of zero articles about Facebook censoring a rabbi who reported antisemitic harassment. Fox News was the only prominent national media outlet to cover the story at all, after the *Jewish Journal* broke the news. If the Jewish outlet hadn't reached out to Facebook, would it have ever restored Rabbi Mlotek's post? It's hard to picture. And that's a disturbing thought.

Facebook Election Ads

Facebook's enforcement of its rules on political advertisements in the 2018 election was one-sided and selective, as well. Facebook dinged an ad from President Trump about illegal immigration because it allegedly violated Facebook's policy against "sensational content." Yet the social media giant had no issue with left-wing billionaire Tom Steyer running political ads that explicitly compared the president to mass-murdering tyrants like Saddam Hussein, Hugo Chavez, and Kim Jong Un.[54] Sensational content isn't "sensational" if Facebook's speech police agree with it.

Facebook also pledged to combat misinformation in its political advertisements, but it had no reservations about accepting the North Dakota Democratic Party's targeted advertisements containing blatant misinformation meant to trick hunters—a group more likely to vote Republican—into sitting out the election. The party created a Facebook page called "Hunter Alerts," designed to look like an apolitical informational page for hunters. The Democrats then bought ads for "Hunter Alerts" that advised hunters not to vote: "ATTENTION HUNTERS: If you vote in North Dakota, you may forfeit hunting licenses you have in other states. If you want to keep your out-of-state hunting licenses, you may not want to vote in North Dakota." The claim was indisputably false, but Facebook only flagged the ads after the Democratic Party discontinued them in the face of public pressure.

Following the 2018 midterm elections, I identified hundreds of misleading Facebook advertisements in which left-wing operatives posed as disgruntled conservatives and encouraged Republicans not to vote in the elections.[55] American Engagement Technologies (AET), founded by former Obama administration official Mikey Dickerson, bought ads for two Facebook pages, "The Daily Real" and "Today's Nation," that encouraged Republican voters to stay home in the midterm elections. Both pages were apparently designed to give the impression that they were operated by frustrated conservatives rather than by Democratic operatives. The American flag-adorned pages encouraged conservative voters to either stay home in November or vote for Democrats to punish Republicans for being insufficiently conservative. Other ads called polls predicting a "blue wave" in the 2018 elections "unreliable" and downplayed the election's importance. The misleading ads collectively garnered millions of impressions. While reporting the story, I asked Facebook whether the misleading political advertisements violated its rules, but only received a response two days after I published the story, at which point Facebook spokesman Devon Kearns assured me that he was "looking into this," but "unfortunately" he wouldn't have a response in time for my deadline (which Facebook had already missed). I replied that regardless of the timing of the company's answer, I would still appreciate a response whenever he could offer clarification on the misleading ads. Despite repeated follow-ups, Kearns never got back to me. Draw your own conclusions.

Facebook Betting on AI

Zuckerberg and other executives have admitted that Facebook is counting on artificial intelligence (AI) to enforce its speech policing.[56] Silicon Valley insiders I spoke to were deeply skeptical that AI could better police "hate speech" than people. If the company can't figure out what's hate speech and what isn't using human censors, it will be considerably more difficult for the company to teach AI to accomplish the (oftentimes nuanced) task, those insiders told me. The end result, they said, will be algorithms erring on the side of censorship, and Facebook will have an easy rebuttal against charges of political bias: it's not us doing the censoring, it's just the algorithm.

Facebook's Supreme Court of Speech

Similarly, Facebook hopes to deflect any blame for censorship by creating a sort of "Supreme Court" to oversee its speech policing on the site. As Zuckerberg told left-wing website *Vox* in April 2018:

> [W]hat I'd really like to get to is an independent appeal. So maybe folks at Facebook make the first decision based on the community standards that are outlined, and then people can get a second opinion. You can imagine some sort of structure, almost like a Supreme Court, that is made up of independent folks who don't work for Facebook, who ultimately make the final judgment call on what should be acceptable speech in a community that reflects the social norms and values of people all around the world.[57]

The beauty of this system for Facebook is that it could both choose the members of this Supreme Court and deny any responsibility for their decisions.

Shifting responsibility is important for Facebook, because it would help it avoid such embarrassing incidents as its censorship of the *Liberty County Vindicator*. The *Vindicator* has served as the local newspaper for the residents of Liberty, Texas, (population 9,215), since 1887. Leading up to July 4, 2018, the *Vindicator* divided the

Declaration of Independence into a series of twelve Facebook posts, posting one per day. On July 2, the tenth day of the *Vindicator*'s series, Facebook removed the post. As the Texan paper dryly informed its readers: "Somewhere in paragraphs twenty-seven to thirty-one of the Declaration of Independence, Thomas Jefferson wrote something that Facebook finds offensive."[58] Only after the *Vindicator* published an article on the censored founding document did Facebook restore its post, which it once again chalked up to an inadvertent mistake. The offending paragraphs contained some of American revolutionaries' grievances against the King of England:

> *He has abdicated Government here, by declaring us out of his Protection and waging War against us.*

> *He has plundered our seas, ravaged our Coasts, burnt our towns, and destroyed the lives of our people.*

> *He is at this time transporting large Armies of foreign Mercenaries to compleat the works of death, desolation and tyranny, already begun with circumstances of Cruelty & perfidy scarcely paralleled in the most barbarous ages, and totally unworthy the Head of a civilized nation.*

> *He has constrained our fellow Citizens taken Captive on the high Seas to bear Arms against their Country, to become the executioners of their friends and Brethren, or to fall themselves by their Hands.*

> *He has excited domestic insurrections amongst us, and has endeavoured to bring on the inhabitants of our*

*frontiers, the merciless Indian Savages, whose known
rule of warfare, is an undistinguished destruction of all
ages, sexes and conditions.*

"While the *Vindicator* cannot be certain exactly what triggered
Facebook's filtering program, the editor suspects it was most likely
the phrase 'Indian Savages,'" the paper's managing editor, Casey
Stinnett, informed readers. "Perhaps had Thomas Jefferson written
it as 'Native Americans at a challenging stage of cultural development'
that would have been better." Stinnett and the *Vindicator* handled
the incident well, but that they had to handle anything at all only
underscores the disturbing extent to which Facebook has already
embraced its role as a global censor and enforcer of political correctness. If posting America's founding documents to Facebook requires
going through an appeal process, we're already squarely in Orwellian
territory.

Facebook's changes to its rules about employees' conduct provide
an illuminating glimpse into the future. The company issued a memo
in January 2019 banning employees from trying to change each others' minds about politics or religion.[59] "We're keeping it simple with
three main guidelines: Don't insult, bully, or antagonize others. Don't
try to change someone's politics or religion. Don't break our rules
about harassing speech and expression," Facebook chief technology
officer Mike Schroepfer wrote in the memo.[60] "These guidelines apply
to all work communications including Workplace, email, chat, tasks,
posters, whiteboards, chalkboards, and face-to-face," Schroepfer
added. "Since Workplace is where most of these discussions happen,
we are investing engineering resources there." If Facebook can't figure
out how to have civil discussion within its own workplace without
cries for censorship, it can't possibly make it work on a platform with
1.25 billion daily active users.[61] Knowledgeable Facebook sources

predict that its speech policies for employees will become its speech policies for users, and controversial opinions—as defined by left-wing activists—will simply be off-limits.

CHAPTER FOUR

One Nation under Google

Google has amassed more power, on a global scale, than any corporation in the history of the world. The tech behemoth and its subsidiary, YouTube, provide the results for more than ninety percent of searches for information on the Internet.[1] "Google" has become a verb, synonymous with "research." If you're looking for an article, you Google it. If you want information about a political candidate, you Google it. If you want to know more about Google itself, you Google it. And to locate a video, you turn to Google-owned YouTube. Google's control of the flow of information—including information about politics and culture—throughout the world is unprecedented. Even more disturbing is the fact that Google is openly moving towards censorship while remaining opaque about how that censorship occurs.

The news itself flows through Google. Media companies depend on Google—both Google News and Google Search—for a sizable portion of their online traffic. The data analytics firm Parse.ly maintains a monthly list of the top "referrers" of online articles. Every month, one referrer stands head and shoulders above the rest: Google's search engine. Google Search drove 30.1 percent of article referrals in December 2018, according to Parse.ly. That was more than double its closest competitor, Facebook, which drove 14.5 percent of article referrals.[2] The third highest: Google News, with 2.3 percent. No other referrer had more than two percent of the market.

"I want you to imagine walking into a room, a control room with a bunch of people, a hundred people, hunched over a desk with little dials, and that that control room will shape the thoughts and feelings of a billion people. This might sound like science fiction, but this actually exists right now, today," former Google design ethicist Tristan Harris said in an April 2017 TED Talk.[3] "I know because I used to be in one of those control rooms. I was a design ethicist at Google, where I studied how do you ethically steer people's thoughts? Because what we don't talk about is how the handful of people working at a handful of technology companies through their choices will steer what a billion people are thinking today," Harris said. When Google is seeking to "ethically" steer thoughts, it matters a heck of a lot what Google employees think is ethical—and what thoughts they want you to think.

Robert Epstein, a senior research psychologist at the American Institute for Behavioral Research and Technology, has studied how Google's search results and recommendations shape users' political opinions. In a study of 661 participants from forty-nine states and ranging in age from eighteen to thirty-five, Epstein found that Google's "SSE ['Search Suggestion Effect'] appears to have the power to change a 50/50 split in preferences among people who are undecided on an issue to a 90/10 split."[4] According to the study, "it is possible that the outcomes of upwards of 25 percent of the world's national elections are now being determined by Google's search algorithm, even without deliberate manipulation on the part of company employees." Based on this data, Epstein and his colleagues concluded that Google's search algorithm "almost certainly ends up favoring one candidate over another in most political races, and that shifts opinions and votes." Epstein's research was prominently featured in the documentary film *The Creepy Line*, which explored Google's ability to manipulate thoughts—and elections.

Google doesn't even need to go so far as downranking specific results about candidates for it to steer users' views towards one candidate and away from another. Thanks to the dependable left-wing biases of corporate media companies like CNN and the *Washington Post*, Google only needs to downrank certain *outlets* that don't conform to the left-wing narrative, and the outcome will be much the same. The political left know this—it's why they've pressured Google to take those very measures.

Google's employees are well aware of their own power, as evidenced by leaked internal discussions on how best to wield that power against conservatives. Google's workplace culture is dominated, top to bottom, by an obsession with left-wing identity politics, lavishing praise on internal teams with a majority of women, and shaming and denigrating internal teams with a majority of men.[5] Google incentivizes employees' attendance at what it calls "anti-bias sessions" where presenters lecture employees on white male privilege.[6] (A 2017 study by Altheas Nagai at the Center for Equal Opportunity found that such sessions are ineffective at best,[7] and there is some data suggesting that they may in fact be counterproductive.[8]) PowerPoint slides from a "Bias Busting" session listed as off-limits: "Debating whether bias exists at your organization."[9] Employees are expected to attend the re-education sessions in order to demonstrate their commitment to diversity and inclusion—though of course it's neither real diversity nor real inclusion. At Google, diversity doesn't apply to diversity of thought, and inclusion doesn't apply to orthodox Christians or social conservatives. Diversity at Google means that managers explicitly try to fill quotas that label employees by race and sex. "Diverse" job candidates—non-white people (except for Asians)—are placed in special queues for priority hiring.[10.] "I could care less about being 'unfair' to white men. You already have all the advantages in the world," one Google employee wrote on an internal message board.[11] Opposing different standards for different races, another employee wrote, is a "microaggression."[12] Another employee claimed that Republicans had declared "war" on her by voting for Trump.[13]

Lower and mid-level employees pressure executives to do more for left-wing causes, both personally and in their professional capacities. I obtained internal Google documents showing that after Trump's election, some Google employees used the company's internal message boards to call for a company-wide boycott of all Trump hotels and Trump-linked businesses. "I think that if Google's company philosophy is to promote inclusion, then to continue to support Trump business endeavors, which are explicitly non-inclusive, would be very contrary to this mission," one employee explained. It was a popular idea. Google's left-wing activists have only gotten bolder with time. More than 1,100 Google employees signed an open letter in November 2019 demanding that the company voluntarily adopt essentially its own version of Ocasio-Cortez's Green New Deal.[14] Under the demanded terms, Google would have to somehow reduce its carbon emissions to zero by the year 2030. The company would also have to boycott any "contracts to enable or accelerate the extraction of fossil fuels."

"Google's culture has many similatiries to the culture of academia, so it's hardly surprising that the outrage mobs (and other trends on college campuses) have caught on much faster at Google," former Google engineer Mike Wacker told me. "It used to be that you would only hear buzzwords and abstract theories such as privilege, critical theory, and intersectionality in the left-wing corners of academia. Now, these ideas have become prevalent at Google. They are often taught as if they are the truth, not just one possible theory, and they have even found their way into documents about performance management," Wacker added.

Some aspects of the company's internal culture could be mistaken for parodies of left-wing campus culture. It's pervaded with snooty elitism and childish temper tantrums. One Google employee from West Virginia recounted conversations denigrating West Virginians and advocating against poor people having children.[15] Sources provided me with internal documents showing Google employees having full-fledged meltdowns about the use of the word "family"—which was presumed to be offensive to people without children. One employee stormed out of a March 2017 meeting when a speaker "continued to show (awesome) Unicorn product features which continually use the word 'family' as a synonym for 'household with children.'" The employee posted an extended rant, which was well-received by his colleagues, on why linking families to children is "offensive, inappropriate, homophobic, and wrong."

> This is a diminishing and disrespectful way to speak. If you mean "children," say "children"; we have a perfectly good word for it. "Family friendly" used as a synonym for "kid friendly" means, to me, "you and yours don't count as a family unless you have children." And while kids may often be less aware of it, there are kids without families too, you know.
>
> The use of "family" as a synonym for "with children" has a long-standing association with deeply homophobic organizations. This does not mean we should not use the word "family" to refer to families, but it means we must doggedly insist that family does not imply children.
>
> Even the sense, "suitable for the whole family," which you might think is unobjectionable, is totally wrong too. It

only works if we have advance shared conception of what "the whole family" is, and that is almost always used to mean a household with two adults, of opposite sex, in a romantic/sexual relationship, with two or more of their own children. If you mean that as a synonym for "suitable for all people" stop and notice the extraordinary unlikelihood of such a thought! So "suitable for the whole family" doesn't mean "all people," it means "all people in families," which either means that all those other people aren't in families, or something even worse. Use the word "family" to mean a loving assemblage of people who may or may not live together and may or may not include people of any particular age. STOP using it to mean "children." It's offensive, inappropriate, homophobic, and wrong.

Roughly one hundred other Google employees "upvoted" that post, signaling their approval for the rant. Some employees echoed their displeasure with the term. "Thanks for writing this. So much yes," one employee agreed. "Using the word 'family' in this sense bothers me too," wrote another employee, who felt excluded by the term because she was neither married nor a parent. "It smacks of the 'family values' agenda by the right wing, which is absolutely homophobic by its very definition," she wrote, adding that "it's important that we fix our charged language when we become aware of how exclusionary it actually is. As a straight person in a relationship, I find the term 'family' offensive because it excludes me and my boyfriend, having no children of our own." Another wrote: "My family consists of me and several other trans feminine folks, some of whom I'm dating. We're all supportive of each other and eventually aspire to live together. Just because we aren't a heterosexual couple with 2.5 kids, a white picket fence, and a dog doesn't mean we're not a family."

Yet another employee wrote that "using 'family' to mean 'people with kids' is also annoying to me as a straight-cis-woman who doesn't have or want kids. My husband, my parents, and my pets are my family." Another: "As someone [aromantic-asexual] (and thus both perpetually, intentionally single and unlikely to ever have a child) I appreciate this being pointed out. My family is not incomplete because it has no children and will never have romantic (or more) relationships. It's incredibly frustrating to constantly run into assumptions that being single and childless is an undesirable, incomplete state—even if those assumptions are implicit and from various statements about what families look like." Google vice president Pavni Diwanji then joined the conversation and acknowledged that the use of the term "family" had sparked "concerns." "Hi everyone, I realize what we said at tgif might have caused concerns in the way we talked about families. There are families without kids too, and also we needed to be more conscientious about the fact that there is a diverse makeup of parents and families," Diwanji wrote. "Please help us get to a better state. Teach us how to talk about it in an inclusive way, if you feel like we are not doing it well. As a team we have a very inclusive culture, and want to do right in this area. I am adding my team here so we can have open conversation," Dwiwanji concluded.

One Google employee, who identifies as both "a yellow-scaled wingless dragonkin" and "an expansive ornate building," gave a PowerPoint presentation at a company event on the topic of "Living as a Plural Being." Slides from the presentation included instructions on how to interact with such a "plural being" without offending them. "Generally plural beings prefer they or you&/your& pronouns, and self-address as we/our," one slide explained. The slide noted that "many of us are stealth," keeping their "plural" identities a secret. At the same time, if you're speaking to a "plural being," it's considered offensive to only address one of their plural identities (referred to as "headmates"). "Addressing any headmate in particular" was listed as an example of problematic office etiquette. "We're all listening," the slide explained. Assuming that people who identify as multiple beings in one body are "mentally damaged" is also a no-no: "actually we're happier this way," the slide stated.[16]

It's important to keep in mind: the people offended by the word "family" are the same ones whose product you trust for accurate answers when you type in: "what is a family?" The people who think a person can identify as "an expansive ornate building" and a "yellow-scaled wingless dragonkin" plural being are the same people whose product you trust to give you an accurate answer to questions like: "what is a man?" or "what is a person?"

Google employees melted down when Trump won. Frustration and dejectedness are normal reactions when your preferred candidate loses an election, but Trump's victory caused more than just those feelings in Silicon Valley. For Google employees, November 2016 sparked an existential crisis. In retrospect, perhaps that should have been no surprise. When your framework for perceiving the world is one in which a society steadily marches leftwards towards an end-of-history type of political utopia, Donald Trump winning an election simply doesn't compute. The reality TV star whose signature campaign promise was building a wall to prevent illegal immigration became president of the United States. That's not supposed to happen. So, after the election, Google held an internal meeting to cope with the tragedy and for many employees, to begin remedying it.

"We have no idea what direction this country will take....It's a period of great uncertainty...especially for immigrants or minorities [and] women," Google co-founder Sergey Brin told employees at an internal meeting. "As an immigrant and a refugee, I certainly find this election deeply offensive, and I know many of you do too."[17] Brin acknowledged at the meeting that "most people here are pretty upset and pretty sad," and said Trump's election "conflicts with many of [Google's] values." Google vice president Kent Walker explained Trump supporters' votes by saying that "fear, not just in the United States but around the world, is fueling concerns, xenophobia, hatred, and a desire for answers that may or may not be there." The video showed Google CFO Ruth Porat apparently reduced to tears at Trump's election. Porat instructed employees in attendance to hug one another, explaining: "we all need a hug." Here's how Allum Bokhari, the reporter who obtained and published that video, described another scene:

> A Google employee states: "speaking to white men, there's an opportunity for you right now to understand your privilege" and urges employees to "go through the bias-busting training, read about privilege, read about the real history of oppression in our country." He urges employees to "discuss the issues you are passionate about during Thanksgiving dinner and don't back down and laugh it off when you hear the voice of oppression speak through metaphors." Every executive on stage—the CEO, CFO, two VPs and the two Co-founders—applaud the employee.[18]

The video is a perfect illustration of how many Google employees interpreted Trump's election: a terrible outcome that they should have done more to prevent the American people from choosing and something they would work hard to make sure didn't happen again. Indeed, I obtained documents and communications showing Google employees organizing anti-Trump protests using internal company channels, company time, and company office space. "If your stomach turns when you consider a Trump presidency, I urge you not to let this moment pass quietly," one Google employee wrote in an email to coworkers, urging them to attend an anti-Trump protest in San Francisco ten days after Trump's election.

Another Google employee in March 2017 hosted an anti-Trump resistance event at Google to flood the White House mail room with anti-Trump postcards. "Hi all," the email began, "I'm participating in #TheIdesofTrump, a national movement to send POTUS a postcard on March 15 expressing opposition to him." The message stated that employees had reserved a room at Google's San Francisco headquarters for Google employees to gather and write the anti-Trump postcards. The invitation included the anti-Trump activists' mission statement:

> We the people, in vast numbers, from all corners of the world, will overwhelm the man in his unpopularity and failure. We will show the media and the politicians what standing with him—and against us—means. And most importantly, we will bury the White House in pink slips, all informing Donnie that he's fired. Each of us—every protester from every march, each congress calling citizen, every boycotter, volunteer, donor, and petition signer—if each of us writes even a single postcard and we put them all in the mail on the same day, March 15th, well: you do the math.
>
> No alternative fact or Russian translation will explain away our record-breaking, officially-verifiable, warehouse-filling flood of fury.

"I'll bring the postcards and the stamps," the employee added. "You just bring your woke selves."

It bears repeating that the employees used their work email addresses, a company listserv, and company office space to organize their anti-Trump activism, because there is absolutely no chance that a Google employee could get away with organizing pro-Trump activism using Google resources on company time. If someone tried, their coworkers would run them out of the company, if their bosses didn't fire them first.

One Google employee even reported a colleague to human resources for supporting Jordan Peterson's objection to state-mandated pronoun laws in Canada. "One Googler raised a concern that you appeared to be promoting and defending Jordan Peterson's comments about transgender pronouns, and expressed concern that this made them feel unsafe at work," HR told the employee in an email, which noted that other Google employees were also "offended by [your] perceived challenge to our diversity programs."

Google engineer James Damore wrote a now-famous memo in August 2017 criticizing the left-wing hivemind at Google. Damore's memo, titled "Google's Ideological Echo Chamber," advocated for viewpoint diversity within the company. "Google's left bias has created a politically correct monoculture that maintains its hold by shaming dissenters into silence. This silence removes any checks against encroaching extremist and authoritarian policies," Damore wrote. Debate and consideration of alternative viewpoints, he argued, are necessary for arriving at truth. Damore used the left-wing consensus on why the number of women working in the tech sector is so low as an example. The left-wing consensus at Google is that there are more males than female working in the tech industry solely because of sexism and implicit biases, but Damore offered an alternative explanation that he thought worthy of consideration. (It's important to note that his answer didn't say that sexist bias was imaginary or a non-factor, but rather argued that other factors were at play *as well*.) Damore's "controversial" argument was that "men and women biologically differ in many ways" as a result of evolution and that those biological differences play a role in what jobs men and women choose to work. Women, he offered in example, are on average more prone to anxiety but also more teamwork-oriented than men (two claims that are supported by scientific research on the subject).[19]

Citing the fact that there are biological differences between men and women in a company-wide discussion about why men and women end up on different career paths isn't unreasonable. It certainly doesn't make the speaker a fascist or a sexist. At worst it might be socially awkward, but let's be real—if social awkwardness was a fireable offense, Silicon Valley would become a ghost town pretty quickly. Damore's whole point was that Googlers would be better served by listening to one another and considering more than one viewpoint on issues rather than reflexively attacking dissenters, and that viewpoint diversity was not valued within the company. And Damore's colleagues wasted no time proving him right.

Google employees became obsessed with getting Damore fired. They launched frenzied attacks against him, with one objective: ridding themselves of the heretic in their midst. A Google director sent a mass email attacking Damore for his "repulsive and intellectually dishonest" memo.[20] Another employee demanded the company not only fire Damore but also punish anyone who voiced their support for him. "If Google management cares enough about diversity and inclusion, they should, and I urge them to, send a clear message by not only terminating Mr. Damore, but also severely disciplining or terminating those who have expressed support" for him, the employee wrote.[21] One engineer at the company emailed Damore pledging all-out war. "You're a misogynist and a terrible person," the engineer wrote. "I will keep hounding you until one of us is fired. Fuck you," he added, daring Damore to "pass this along to HR."[22] Damore did pass it along to Google's HR department, and the department responded by instructing him to work from home. Google then fired him for "perpetuating gender stereotypes."[23] Damore became a pariah in Silicon Valley and eventually moved to Texas to try to start his life over.

"When Damore presented his ideas for increasing female participation in tech, he precipitated an internal lynch mob at Google. The participants' behavior was frightening," one politically moderate employee said in hindsight. "Some switch flipped and they were acting like deranged lunatics, as if they had experienced terrible traumas instead of working at one of the richest and [most] generous companies in the world."[24] A conservative tech employee added: "James Damore's firing was a huge wake-up call. Silicon Valley has been for my career left-liberal, but now it makes me wonder if we've moved from live and let live to an environment where if you don't go along with the prevailing politics you're out of a livelihood."[25]

Former Google employee David Gudeman said he, too, lost his job because he broke with political consensus inside the company. Gudeman sparked a backlash after Trump's election by accusing hysterical coworkers of being stuck in a liberal bubble. Anyone "who believes President Trump will be out to get minorities, women or gays has absorbed a lot of serious lies from their echo chamber. And the echo chamber is entirely one sided," Gudeman wrote in an internal post. At the time, Gudeman was working at Google as an engineer. "You can't watch TV or go to movies without being constantly confronted with the leftist worldview. Leftists can go their whole life never being exposed to the conservative worldview except in shows written by people hostile to it," Gudeman wrote. One of Gudeman's colleagues said he was afraid after Trump's election because he was "already targeted by the FBI" for being a Muslim. Gudeman reacted skeptically. He wondered: was President Barack Obama's Department of Justice really racially profiling a Muslim Google employee? Gudeman was fired shortly afterwards.[26]

One conservative Google employee was scolded for responding to a thread specifically asking for conservative parenting advice. The employee had written: "If I had a child, I would teach him/her traditional gender roles and patriarchy from a very young age. That's the hardest thing to fix later, and our degenerate society constantly pushes the wrong message." Google's internal speech cops couldn't let that pass. Google HR sent him a warning email, though they admitted he didn't break any rules: "We did not find that this post, on its face, violated any of Google's policies, but your choice of words could suggest that you were advocating for a system in which men work outside the home and women do not, or that you were advocating for rigid adherence to gender identity at birth. We trust that neither is what you intended to say," read the less-than-subtle email. "In other words, Google scolded the Google Employee for, among other things, believing that gender identity is set at birth biologically—a position held by the vast majority of the world's populace that Google professes to serve," California attorney Harmeet Dhillon wrote in a lawsuit on behalf of Damore, Gudeman, and other former Google employees who said they had been targeted for their political beliefs. The lawsuit included screenshots of Google employees bragging on internal forums about blacklisting conservative employees and interns from hiring pools.[27] "I will never, ever hire/transfer you onto my team. Ever. I don't care if you are perfect fit or technically excellent or whatever. I will actively not work with you, even to the point where your team or product is impacted by this decision. I'll communicate why to your manager if it comes up," one manager wrote on an internal forum, referring to conservatives and other "hostile voices." Another "publicly bragged about blacklisting an intern for failing to change his conservative views," the suit noted. "The primary purpose of these blacklists and suggested blacklists was to encourage and coordinate the sabotage of promotions, performance reviews, and employment opportunities for those with conservative viewpoints," Dhillon wrote.

Leftist Big Tech employees' silencing of political dissent within their ranks is important for at least two reasons. First, it's evidence that left-wing ideologues at tech companies are willing to use their power to silence political dissent. Where they have power, they wield it against conservatives and others who challenge progressive tenets. Second, by silencing and forcing out non-leftists, Big Tech is ridding itself of the people most willing to object to the company's bias. In other words: the blind spots will only get bigger; the bias will only get worse; and that will only become more important as tech companies take on ever greater roles as ideological gatekeepers—a role they already see themselves adopting. A March 2018 internal Google memo explained that on the Internet, free speech is problematic because "free speech becomes a social, economic and political weapon."[28] So tech companies had to impose censorship.[29] "Although people have long been racist, sexist and hateful in many other ways," the memo stated, "they weren't [previously] empowered by the internet...." Censoring such voices was the right thing to do in order to ease "the anxiety of users and governments." According to internal Google communications I reviewed, Google employees openly debated whether to bury conservative media outlets such as the Daily Caller and Breitbart in the company's search function after Donald Trump's election as president. The documents show Google employees discussing ways Google could prevent Trump from winning again—in particular by exerting greater control over what information Google's users would see. "This was an election of false equivalencies, and Google, sadly, had a hand in it," Google engineer Scott Byer wrote in a November 9, 2016, post. Byer mischaracterized the Daily Caller and Breitbart as "opinion blogs" and urged his coworkers to reduce their visibility in sections of Google's search results pertaining to electoral information. "How many times did you see…items from opinion blogs (Breitbart, Daily Caller) elevated next to legitimate news organizations? That's something that can and should be fixed," Byer wrote. "I think we have a responsibility to expose the quality and truthfulness of sources—because not doing so hides real information under loud noises," he continued. "Beyond that, let's concentrate on teaching critical thinking. A little bit of that would go a long way. Let's make sure that we reverse things in four years—demographics will be on our side." It doesn't take a lot of parsing to figure out what "Let's make sure that we reverse things in four years" means. It's an explicit call to leverage Google's influence to affect presidential election outcomes.

The internal conversation revealed a more pernicious aspect of online censorship as well. Some of Byer's colleagues, including a Google vice president, didn't voice opposition to his goal of changing the company's policies and methods for the purpose of affecting an election outcome. Instead, they only disagreed with his tactics. Their solution: subtle censorship. "We're working on providing users with context around stories so that they can know the bigger picture," engineering vice president David Besbris wrote in a reply. "We can play a role in providing the full story and educate them about all sides. This doesn't have to be filtering and can be useful to everyone." Other employees sounded similar notes. Burying specific media outlets had the potential to backfire. It was better instead to first provide context about media outlets. The inevitable tension would be in deciding which outlets people should trust and which ones they shouldn't, and what context they needed to help tell the difference. But that's nothing an ideological echo chamber can't handle. Google later implemented a program that closely followed the subtler option floated by Besbris and others.

In January 2017, after President Trump announced his initial "travel ban" (an executive order to temporarily restrict entry of travelers from certain countries to the United States), Google employees brainstormed ways to counter "islamophobic, algorithmically biased results from search terms 'Islam', 'Muslim', 'Iran', etc," as well as "prejudiced, algorithmically biased search results from search terms 'Mexico', 'Hispanic', 'Latino', etc."[30] In February 2017, Google employees pushed to kick Breitbart out of its program Adsense, citing "hate speech." The employees supported the work of Sleeping Giants, a left-wing group trying to defund Breitbart through ad boycotts.[31]

Google and YouTube's special favors for what they deem "authoritative content" is really a form of protectionism for the liberal establishment. When 95 percent of Google users don't click past the first page of results,[32] Google can pretty much dictate the answers to a user's questions. In April 2017, Google began a massive restructuring of its search algorithms. Google "adjusted our signals to help surface more authoritative pages and demote low-quality content," company vice president Ben Gomes wrote in a blog post announcing the change. In March 2018, Google made a similar change to its Google News function, placing greater weight on "authoritative content." Google employees' internal conversations leave little doubt about which publications Google employees think are authoritative (liberal publications) and which they think aren't (non-liberal publications).

YouTube in July 2018 announced an overhaul to its search algorithm that would "prominently surface authoritative sources" on certain topics.[33] When Google and YouTube say they're going to "prominently surface authoritative sources," what they mean is they're going to boost liberal establishment media outlets like CNN higher in the search results while making right-of-center outlets and conservative viewpoints harder to find. What this means in practice is if you search for "gay wedding cake" on YouTube, looking for insight on the religious freedom battle being fought in the courts about whether a Christian baker can be forced to violate his conscience, all of the top results will be from "authoritative sources," including a skit from liberal late night host Jimmy Kimmel, which isn't authoritative at all. He completely butchers the details of the case and misleads his viewers.[34] A video in which conservative comedian Steven Crowder requests gay wedding cakes from Muslim bakers (and is turned down), is nowhere near the front page,[35] despite having a staggering 6.7 million views, by far the most views on the subject.[36] The next most popular video on the topic: a Ben Shapiro interview with Dave Rubin, a gay, liberal YouTube host who defends the right of Christian bakers to follow their consciences. That video, too, has millions of views, but is nowhere near the front page. The third most popular video is a clip from *The View* in which actress Candace Cameron Bure defended the bakers. It's nowhere near the front page, either.

Likewise, when I search for "transgender bathrooms," the top results are two-year-old news clips, many of which have garnered fewer than 100,000 views. Ben Shapiro has multiple videos on the subject with view counts in the millions. Once again, they're buried far away from the first page of search results.

According to internal Google communications and documents I obtained, in June 2018, upset Google employees succeeded in banning an advertisement for a video that explained Christian teaching on marriage. The video was flagged in an internal listserv, "Yes at Google," which is run by Google's human resources department. The listserv has more than 30,000 members and is devoted to policing "microaggressions" and "micro-corrections" within the company, according to its official internal description. A Google vice president assured angry employees that the video would no longer run as an advertisement.

In the video, Christian radio host Michael L. Brown welcomed gay Christians but said they are called to follow the same Christian teachings on sex and marriage. In the video, he describes same-sex relationships as "like other sins, but one that Jesus died for." Brown, it's worth noting, is no extremist on the issue; he has spoken out against the Westboro Baptist Church's hateful rhetoric against gay people; and the belief that sexual relationships are meant to take place in the context of a marriage between one man and one women—as argued by Brown—is central to most major Christian denominations' marital teachings. But those teachings are unconscionable at Google. Google HR highlighted in the listserv a "representative" comment from an employee who took offense that Brown's video had appeared as an advertisement on channels operated by gay and lesbian YouTubers. "I cannot see how this can be allowed when the specific idea of LGBT videos is to allow the creators to feel free to share their content and be comfortable that anti-LGBT advertisers would not be attached to their content," the employee wrote. "This seems very counter to our mission, specifically around PRIDE 2018 timeframe." Google's vice president for product management and ads, Vishal Sharma, agreed that the video was too offensive to air as an advertisement. "Thank you for raising this very important issue. It means a lot to me personally and those of us working on this across the Ads and You-Tube teams. YouTube is an open platform, and we support the free expression of creators with a wide range of views," Sharma wrote in his response, which was included in the listserv. "But we don't allow advertising that disparages people based on who they are—including their sexual orientation—and we remove ads that violate this basic principle," Sharma continued. "After careful and multiple reviews over the course of a few days, our teams decided to remove the ad in question here as it violates our policy. We've communicated this to the advertiser and have been in touch with creators who have been actively engaged on this issue," he added, again expressing his gratitude for Google employees' bringing this matter to his attention.

YouTube's censorship of a video produced by the Daily Signal, the media arm of The Heritage Foundation, offers a clear example of how the company's step-by-step approach to censorship is choking out conservative speech on the most important issues of our time. The Daily Signal released a video in December 2017 featuring Dr. Michelle Cretella, a longtime pediatrician and executive director of the American College of Pediatricians. Cretella laid out straightforward, scientific facts, like: "Biological sex is not assigned. Sex is determined at conception by our DNA and is stamped into every cell of our bodies."[37] "If you want to cut off a leg or an arm you're mentally ill, but if you want to cut off healthy breasts or a penis, you're transgender." For over a year, the video remained up on YouTube with no issue—and why shouldn't it have? After all, a medical professional providing a medical opinion on an important topic is the kind of "authoritative content" YouTube is supposed to be prioritizing. But of course the whole point of YouTube retooling its platform was to enforce the liberal establishment's point of view. So the video had to go. YouTube pulled the video in 2019, citing one sentence from the video, in which Cretella said: "See, if you want to cut off a leg or an arm, you're mentally ill, but if you want to cut off healthy breasts or a penis, you're transgender."[38] It's an objectively true statement—but it's not allowed on YouTube.

■   ■   ■

In a January 25, 2019, blog post, YouTube announced the company would be "taking a closer look at how we can reduce the spread of content that comes close to—but doesn't quite cross the line of—violating our Community Guidelines." Like Facebook's algorithm change, this shift means punishing content that's not actually breaking the rules. "To that end, we'll begin reducing recommendations of borderline content and content that could misinform users in harmful ways—such as videos promoting a phony miracle cure for a serious illness, claiming the earth is flat, or making blatantly false claims about historic events like 9/11," the blog post read.[39] YouTube cited alarmist examples like 9/11 "truther" videos as a shield against criticism, but this was a significant step towards manipulating its users. Recommended videos, the ones you see on the homepage and off to the side of whatever video you're watching, are a major eyeball driver on YouTube. They're meant to be similar to what your interests are— but now YouTube is working to redirect your interests if the company deems them harmful, *even if none of the videos in question violates YouTube's rules.* "YouTube is a particularly tragic case in my view, because that was the one area where independent media, even more than Twitter and maybe even more than Facebook, where one-man operations could really rise to prominence, it was sort of like a new talk radio, you could have a small, simple set-up and attract audiences of tens and hundreds of thousands," Allum Bokhari, a prolific tech reporter, told me. "You look at the recent YouTube changes, and they're elevating all these mainstream media outlets, and they're also elevating Fox News as the token conservative, but it's essentially the same situation as the 1990s, where you have all these liberal networks and the one token conservative outlet."

He continued, saying "the idea that YouTube is going to take away that engine of success and that opportunity that was there for millions and millions of people, and just give all the power back to the mainstream media networks that they were originally disrupting is pretty tragic. These tech platforms—they marketed themselves as disruptors, as this new way to reach people. I mean YouTube's slogan is still broadcast yourself, user-created content... but here they are elevating these media empires that already have tons of resources, over their own content creators. One of the videos they downranked was a woman sharing her story of being pressured to get an abortion. It was a perfectly fine video, just one woman's anecdote with hundreds of thousands of views, and there was no reason why that video shouldn't be at the top of the abortion search results, but instead they've replaced it with all these videos from Vice News and BBC and BuzzFeed, and they're giving this special advantage to media outlets that don't deserve it and already have tons of resources anyway. It just makes no sense."

YouTube announced that the initial changes would affect less than one percent of videos on its platform—which even if true, was still an enormous amount of content.[40] Five billion videos are watched on YouTube every single day.[41] If YouTube pulled recommendations to even just half of one percent of those videos, that would be twenty-five million videos every day. And of course, in a June 2019 blog post, YouTube announced that it was expanding the program.[42] This time, YouTube left out how many videos would be affected, simply saying that "even more" videos would be smothered by the algorithms. "Our systems are also getting smarter about what types of videos should get this treatment, and we'll be able to apply it to even more borderline videos moving forward," read the blog post. Which videos exactly are being suppressed? YouTube won't say. You'll just have to take them at their word that they're playing fair. "As we do this, we'll also start raising up more authoritative content in recommendations, building on the changes we made to news last year. For example, if a user is watching a video that comes close to violating our policies, our systems may include more videos from authoritative sources (like top news channels) in the 'watch next' panel," the announcement continued. In other words: YouTube would shove CNN videos down the throats of viewers who strayed too far.

It's not a coincidence that YouTube's algorithm changes have shifted in favor of the corporate media outlets that many YouTube users were trying to escape in the first place. YouTube isn't going to be a place for everyone anymore. It's going to be a place for professional YouTube channels—primarily establishment liberal news organizations. That's not what YouTube was for most of its existence. It's not what made YouTube, YouTube. But that is what is happening.

Between changing its approaches to search results and its format for recommended videos, YouTube is actively picking winners and losers on its platform, driving viewers to some channels and away from others, and promoting some opinions and demoting opposing ones. The big winner: the liberal establishment media. The big losers: conservative and independent channels[43] and small channels that were demonetized.[44]

What YouTube and Google are doing is overriding user choice. Most people searching for "abortion" on YouTube aren't interested in watching a CNN news video—they're looking for information and viewpoints that CNN won't show, which is why pro-life content outperforms pro-abortion content when the playing field is neutral, and why YouTube first became a popular outlet for conservative commentators who dissented from the liberal media establishment. But Google and YouTube are now playing the role of hall monitor, and they are hardly neutral; they have an institutional point of view that is left-wing, and they are working with the liberal establishment media to stifle dissenting conservative voices.

Google announced in April 2017 that it would be placing articles from select fact checkers at the top of search results.[45] The left-leaning sites Snopes and PolitiFact, were among the outlets to receive these special privileges.[46] Snopes already had a track record of hiring left-wing bloggers and publishing slanted fact checks when they began working with Google, and that pattern has only continued. When Snopes botched its fact check of the Covington Catholic controversy, (where students from the school were harassed by a leftist American Indian activist and a black nationalist group called the Black Hebrew

Israelites), Google placed the inaccurate fact check at the top of its search results.

In late 2017, Google expanded the fact check program to provide additional context on media outlets. The plan bore a striking resemblance to what Google vice president David Besbris had proposed in a leaked internal chat: "We're working on providing users with context around stories so that they can know the bigger picture. We can play a role in providing the full story and educate them about all sides." Google's algorithm plugged fact-checks from liberal outlets like Snopes into context bars for media outlets—but not all media outlets. The fact-checking operation targeted right-of-center outlets almost exclusively. It was also blatantly wrong.

Google's fact check repeatedly attributed false claims to conservative outlets, even though they demonstrably never made those claims.[47] It was so bad that fact-checking outlets had to publicly distance themselves from the program, blaming Google for the bad results. Google only pulled the program in January 2018 after an investigation by The Daily Caller News Foundation, my employer, revealed the blatant inaccuracies throughout. Google blamed the faulty fact-checks on a bug in its algorithm, but they still haven't explained why conservative outlets were the ones targeted. Google still privileges select publications like Snopes, giving them top placement in Google Search and Google News.

Censorship can be imposed without banning conservative media outlets or burying them in search results. Another way is by threatening to boycott companies that advertise on conservative media by labeling such media "extremist." Leftwing activists and journalists sometimes join forces on these campaigns. YouTube cut off thousands of accounts from its monetization program beginning in March 2017, after media investigations found ads on YouTube running alongside extremist content. The initial investigation by the *Times* of London focused on content produced by neo-Nazi groups and Islamic extremists,[48] but ensuing coverage from other media outlets labeled pro-life videos as "extremist," and pressured Google to target them as well.[49] The ensuing changes didn't just sweep up ISIS propaganda flagged by media outlets, it shook up the entire YouTube landscape, hurting smaller and independent publishers in the process.

YouTube nearly doubled the size of its "Trusted Flagger" program over the course of 2017, adding fifty government agencies and non-governmental organizations (NGOs) to the program, YouTube public policy director Juniper Downs told a Senate committee in January 2018. YouTube empowers the third-party organizations—"Trusted Flaggers"—to help police content on the platform by mass flagging content and working closely with engineers who design YouTube's algorithms, according to Downs' testimony and my conversations with a YouTube spokeswoman in January 2018.[50] Downs described some of the steps Google had taken at that point to suppress "offensive" or "inflammatory" content that falls short of violating YouTube's rules. "Some borderline videos, such as those containing inflammatory religious or supremacist content without a direct call to violence or a primary purpose of inciting hatred, may not cross these lines for removal. But we understand that these videos may be offensive to many and have developed a new treatment for them," she said. "Identified borderline content will remain on YouTube behind an interstitial, won't be recommended, won't be monetized, and won't have key features including comments, suggested videos, and likes. Initial uses have been positive and have shown a substantial reduction in watch time of those videos."

YouTube's demonetization push was meant to accommodate advertisers who seek to avoid controversial content, the company spokeswoman told me at that time. But the pressure didn't let up. Two months after that conversation, the multinational corporation

Unilever threatened to pull all of its ads from Facebook, Google, and Twitter unless the tech giants ramped up their content moderation. The corporation cited concerns about fake news and hate speech.[51] If placing advertisements on YouTube is now seen as a political statement, then advertisers are going to push for content that's palatable to left-wing activists in order to avoid protests and boycotts and protect their clients. And YouTube will happily comply; in 2018, it was reported that YouTube had, yet again, mistakenly deleted conservative channels from the site.[52] In February 2018, YouTube demonetized a conversation between liberal YouTube host Dave Rubin (a staunch critic of left-wing censorship), Jordan Peterson, and Ben Shapiro. YouTube only reinstated the video after I said I was writing an article about YouTube censorship. YouTube once more blamed faulty algorithms.[53]

Censorship: A PR Decision

Google insists that they have processes in place to prevent political bias from influencing their policies. Individual Google employees can't just demonetize videos, Google tells the public. Reality paints a different picture: Google tailors its demonetization decisions to keep liberal reporters and activists happy. In fact, in court documents filed on December 29, 2017, Google's lawyers emphasized that "Decisions about which videos fall into that [demonetization] category are often complicated and may involve difficult, subjective judgment calls." Indeed.

Internal documents I obtained show the extent to which Google's public relations team quarterbacks the content-policing process. One email exchange shows a Google spokeswoman making snap decisions—in direct response to media inquiries—about which YouTube videos to demonetize and which channels to scrutinize. The catalyst was an email from a reporter from *The Guardian*, a left-leaning British publication, asking about specific videos. The reporter's inquiry was based in part on complaints from the Southern Poverty Law Center (SPLC), a left-wing smear factory. Among the videos the SPLC found problematic was one satirizing gender differences. The Google public relations representative forwarded the email to the censorship team and ordered it to review the videos, "making sure they are not monetized." In other words, censorship decisions are viewed as public relations decisions, not as content decisions. That's not how the process is supposed to work—and it is certainly not how Google says the process works. Public relations representatives are supposed to explain the censorship process—not dictate it to please liberal reporters. The exchange also highlights how left-wing interest groups with an egregious track record of dishonesty (like the SPLC) partner with liberal reporters to pressure big tech to censor right-of-center voices.

The fact that Google maintains a pretense of neutrality while cracking down on right-of-center content is particularly dishonest, considering that Google funds, produces, and promotes left-wing propaganda through its "Creators for Change Program." Google has spent millions of dollars on the program, which gives left-wing YouTubers a boost from the world's most powerful company. That includes left-wing writer Amani Al-Khatahtbeh. Google described her as "a rising voice in social, religious, and political issues" and noted that "Amani was invited by Michelle Obama to speak at the inaugural U.S. State of Women Summit." What YouTube didn't mention is that Amani's past work includes a video claiming the September 11, 2001, Islamist terrorist attacks were "an inside job." While YouTube was cracking down on right-wing accounts in the name of fighting conspiracy theories, the company was funding a 9/11 "truther."[54]

Subhi Taha, a YouTube-sponsored "Creator for Change role model," has similarly promoted anti-Israel boycotts. YouTube and

Taha collaborated on a video about Palestinian refugees—who turned out to be family friends of Taha—that promoted an outrageously one-sided narrative about the Israeli-Palestinian conflict. The video stated as fact that Israel committed genocide against Palestinians, while also leaving out any mention of the actions of Palestinian terrorist groups like Hamas. In fact, to call the video one-sided would be generous. It was genuine anti-Israel propaganda funded, produced, and promoted by YouTube.

In addition to smearing Israel, YouTube spends money promoting open-borders propaganda. The tech giant partnered with Creators for Change "role model" Yasmany Del Real on a video opposing enforcement of U.S. border laws. "I had the opportunity to visit some migrant centers and heard many different stories but with only one goal: to achieve the American dream," Del Real says in the video. "Cesar is just one of many who shares the same goal," he continues, before introducing Cesar: a Guatemalan illegal immigrant with a previous deportation on his record. "I would love for people to have a better sense of compassion towards us immigrants. We truly only want to work and to work hard. Many of us have multiple jobs. We work during the day and evenings," Cesar says, in Spanish. "Many of us only want temporary work, without aspiring to stay permanently in the U.S.A.," Cesar adds, unintentionally undermining the narrator's assertion that every border crosser is only interested in pursuing the American dream and contributing to society. "Cesar is from Guatemala, and this is his second time trying to emigrate to the United States. This time it took him one month to reach the border. Despite the fear and anguish of knowing he could be deported a second time, Cesar remains optimistic," Del Real explains, as the video cuts to Cesar. "The United States is a beautiful country, it is a great place to find employment," Cesar says. In the background, a gospel-style singer croons an open-borders anthem: "*Forgive me for trespassing on your lands/That's not an intention of mine/Family and friends we have left behind/Poverty and destitution are my only crime."*

Maybe you agree with those messages; maybe you don't. That's not the point. These are the kind of videos you might expect from a left-wing advocacy group or media outlet. They are not the kind of videos that a politically neutral company produces. If Google is going to sponsor and produce left-wing, open-borders content, then they should publicly acknowledge that they're an ideologically left-wing company that is promoting left-wing narratives. Indeed, that's what Google is: an ideologically left-leaning company staffed by people who resent the right's success on its massive video platform and are actively working to counter it. At the end of the day, Google agrees with progressive activists that the political left deserves a built-in advantage on its platform. But that doesn't stop them from lying about it.

CHAPTER FIVE

Twitter's Free Speech Farce

Twitter punches above its weight class in terms of driving the national debate, compared to Facebook and Google. The latter companies derive their influence from the sheer force of their size. Twitter has a massive number of users in comparison to many other tech platforms, but it's not nearly as large as Facebook and Google. Twitter has approximately sixty-sixty million active users in the United States every month—roughly half the size of the 2016 presidential electorate.[1]

What distinguishes Twitter from Facebook is *who* uses its platform and *how* they use it. Twitter is upstream of Facebook, in terms of driving the media narrative. In fact, Twitter feeds into pretty much everything else. Stories characterized as "breaking news" on cable networks were "breaking news" on Twitter ten minutes—or sometimes even hours or days—before. Journalists use Twitter to collect basic facts and see how other journalists are covering a story, in addition to promoting their own work. For that reason, Twitter can—and often does—add several layers to the media bubble.

The primary reason President Trump uses Twitter is because it empowers him to drive media narratives in real time. Within thirty seconds of a presidential tweet, journalists are quote-tweeting the latest 280-character missive sent in ALL CAPS from the President of the United States. Ten minutes after Trump hits the send button for a tweet, news organizations have already turned his post into a short blurb with a splashy headline. And ten minutes after that, CNN has already put together a panel of commentators pondering the implications of *this* Trump tweet about a witch hunt. "I can go bing bing bing…and they put it on and as soon as I tweet it out — this morning on television, Fox — 'Donald Trump, we have breaking news'" Trump once recounted.[2]

But the phenomenon is not limited solely to Trump—it's simply a reality of the modern media environment. The quickest way to attract mainstream media attention is to demonstrate that the story is already trending on social media. When something—anything, no matter how dumb—trends nationally on Twitter, it quickly migrates to articles published by national media outlets. If the story itself contains precious little news value, outlets will adopt a news hook along the lines of "X Public Figure Said Y, and Twitter Users Were Not Having It." A key factor that distinguishes Twitter from Facebook is the nature of the *audience* its users are attempting to reach. Most Facebook users intend to communicate with friends, not strangers. Twitter is far more impersonal and far less civilized—and that's its appeal. At its best, Twitter allows individuals to critique and correct media coverage in real time, and even to outflank liberal media outlets when they aren't covering an issue. The Gosnell trial is a perfect example.

Kermit Gosnell is possibly America's most prolific mass murderer.[3] He's also among America's least notorious mass murderers. His atrocities have been buried solely because of his chosen profession: Gosnell is an abortionist. Or rather, he was an abortionist, before he went to prison. He allegedly executed hundreds of fully born infants by snipping their spines outside the womb.[4] The details from his trial were horrific.[5] Fetal remains were scattered over the clinic.[6] The bodies of dead newborns were often left out overnight, one former employee testified. "You knew about it the next day when you opened the door....Because you could smell it as soon as you opened the door," she said.[7] Another employee, who wasn't cleared to practice medicine in an abortion clinic but did so anyway, testified: "It would rain fetuses. Fetuses and blood all over the place." Police found full-term babies and body parts—feet in particular—in jars throughout Gosnell's clinic. Gosnell was an objectively evil man who, by all accounts, took pleasure in his brutality.[8] In one instance, Gosnell reportedly joked about the size of the baby—and he called it a baby—that he was about to murder: "this baby is going to walk me home."[9] But a well-placed snip of Gosnell's scissors made sure the baby would never walk, would never smile, and would never draw another breath of air.

The Gosnell trial was filled with shocking, nauseating anecdotes about an evil man who preyed upon vulnerable women and defenseless infants. But the same media outlets who have since praised themselves for their bravery in the Trump era and labeled themselves Guardians of Truth, wouldn't touch the story with a ten-foot scalpel. When the trial began, the dozens of courtroom seats reserved for journalists were embarrassingly empty. The story only broke into the national media at all because of the efforts of conservatives on Twitter. A pro-life blogger, J.D. Mullane, snapped a picture of the empty courtroom seats and tweeted it out. The media cover-up sparked outrage. More than 100,000 tweets with the hashtag #Gosnell quickly pushed the story into the national eye, despite the national media's best efforts. After days of grassroots public shaming, scores of national media outlets sent reporters to cover the trial. That would never have happened without Twitter, as left-wing journalist

Dave Weigel, now with the *Washington Post*, complained in a Slate article.[10] (Imagine being a journalist and complaining that people are paying attention to a literal serial killer of newborn infants.)

That's the power of Twitter—and that's why the political left is working overtime to control it.

Twitter's Leftists

If employees' political donations are any indication, Twitter is staffed almost exclusively by leftists. Individual Twitter employees gave approximately $228,000 to political candidates in the 2018 midterm elections. Of that $228,000, ninety-nine percent went to Democratic candidates, an analysis by Recode found.[11] Among tech companies, only Netflix had a higher partisan skew among its employees than Twitter. (Recode found that 99.6 percent—100 percent if you're rounding up—of Netflix employees' 2018 campaign donations went to Democrats.)

In 2016, the consensus at Twitter was that Trump would get crushed in the general election.[12] When that didn't happen, Twitter employees had a meltdown, blaming their own company. "Twitter helped in promoting Trump," Twitter engineer Marina Zhao tweeted the day after Trump's election. She claimed that "Twitter helped in spreading falsehoods and lies."[13] She and her colleagues demanded change, and they've gotten it. The fact that Twitter CEO Jack Dorsey shares their beliefs and is firmly in the left-wing camp certainly aids their efforts. In April 2018, Dorsey promoted an article by tech executive Peter Leyden calling for a left-wing victory in what the author called America's "second civil war." Leyden wrote, "In this current period of American politics, at this juncture in our history, there's no way that a bipartisan path provides the way forward. The way forward is on the path California blazed about fifteen years ago. At some point, one side or the other must win—and win big. The side resisting change, usually the one most rooted in the past systems and incumbent interests, must be thoroughly defeated—nor just for a political cycle or two, but for a generation or two.… America can't afford more political paralysis. One side or the other must win. This is a civil war that can be won without firing a shot. But it is a fundamental conflict between two worldviews that must be resolved in short order."[14] Dorsey buys into Leyden's worldview entirely. He is so completely on board with the culture war that two months later, he issued a public apology for eating at Chick-fil-A.[15] He is the Platonic ideal of the Silicon Valley progressive.

The Twitter CEO has worked to distance his company from its former position as the "free speech wing of the free speech party." Twitter senior strategist Nick Pickles compared the platform to a "safe space" in July 2018 congressional testimony. "We want to ensure that Twitter continues to be a safe space for our users to share their viewpoints with the broader Twitter community," said Pickles.[16] In a speech to a WIRED25 media summit in October 2018, Dorsey claimed that the "free speech wing" slogan was actually just one big joke. "This quote around 'free speech wing of the free speech party' was never—was never a mission of the company. It was never a descriptor of the company that we gave ourselves. It was a—it was a joke," Dorsey insisted to the audience, though of course Twitter had publicly fostered that free speech image for years.[17]

Dorsey understands that the left's position on free speech has changed, and as left-wing as Dorsey may be, the people working underneath him are far more extreme. Take Twitter senior manager Ian Brown, for example, who is open about his desire to see Trump—"this motherfucker," as he referred to the president in one tweet—out of the White House and in jail.[18]

Twitter launched its Intersectionality, Culture and Diversity Team (ICD) in September 2017,[19] signaling its solidarity with the ideological far left, reinforcing intersectionality as the company's official religion, and priming employees for activism along intersectional lines.

In November 2017, a Twitter contractor on his last day with the company deleted President Trump's account from the site.[20] Twitter scrambled to restore Trump's account, which went missing for eleven minutes, but it underscored just how much power is at the fingertips of individual employees and contractors.

The Shift

Twitter's speech policing used to be about fighting harassment and "fake news"; now it focuses on combating "unhealthy conversations."

Immediately after the election, Twitter banned a slew of members of the so-called "alt-right," which consists of racist losers and whose national conventions draw about 200 to 300 people—on a good day. For comparison, BronyCon, a convention for male enthusiasts of My Little Pony, draws roughly twenty times that number.[21] So the alt-right is an easy target. But, of course, Twitter didn't care when the alt-right was harassing conservative Jewish journalists. In fact, the alt-right's number one target for antisemitic abuse on Twitter was Ben Shapiro, according to an analysis from the left-leaning Anti-Defamation League.[22] But after Donald Trump's election Twitter went looking for groups to ban, and it didn't stop with the alt-right.

Some of its targets were justifiable. For instance, Twitter vice president Colin Crowell announced in June 2017 that Twitter would begin tackling the problem of fake accounts, or "bots," on the platform. Though the lack of transparency—Crowell insisted that the company's banning criteria had to remain secret to be effective—was worrying.

Then, in October 2017, Twitter rolled out a new initiative to purge content that "glorifies violence." Twitter already prohibited "direct violent threats," "vague violent threats," and "wishes/hopes of serious physical harm, death, or disease." But the change came several months after President Trump tweeted a joke video of him supposedly body-slamming CNN, a video that infuriated his journalist critics.

In March 2018, Dorsey pledged a broad overhaul of speech policing on Twitter. He noted that in the past Twitter had focused most of its efforts on removing content that violated the platform's terms of use. That was no longer enough. Twitter was now focused on "building a systemic framework to help encourage more healthy debate, conversations, and critical thinking," Dorsey announced.[23] Dorsey promised that the company would "commit to a rigorous and independently vetted set of metrics to measure the health of public conversation on Twitter."[24] Twitter was shifting from ejecting rule breakers to monitoring the "healthiness" of tweeted conversations, and sure enough in May 2018, Twitter announced that it was taking steps to fight "bad-faith actors" on the platform, in order to promote "healthy conversation." As senior Twitter strategist Nick Pickles told Congress two months later, the changes would allow Twitter to "more effectively address behaviors and activity on the platform that do not necessarily violate our policies, but that distort and detract from the public conversation."[25] Pickles told Congress that "this approach enables us to improve the overall health of the conversation without needing to remove content from Twitter." Pickles continued: "Ultimately, everyone's comments and perspectives are available, but those who are simply looking to disrupt the conversation will not be rewarded by having their Tweets placed at the top of the conversation or search results."

Much about the new operation remained hidden. Twitter refused to disclose how the operation worked, who would be considered a bad-faith actor, or how it would make that determination. Twitter said the change wasn't political in intent, but it soon became political in effect.

Twitter Shadow-Bans Conservative Users

In July 2018, Vice News, a left-liberal publication, revealed that Twitter was making the accounts of several high-profile Republicans harder to find. The suppressed accounts included four Republican members of Congress and Ronna Romney McDaniel, the chairwoman of the Republican National Committee.[26] Vice News reported that "Democrats are not being 'shadow banned' in the same way," noting: "Not a single member of the 78-person Progressive Caucus" was similarly hidden in Twitter searches.

Twitter didn't penalize the Republican congressmen because they said something offensive, but because the "wrong" accounts were engaging with their tweets, Twitter executives conceded. Apparently, the censored Republicans were guilty of being followed by people deemed "bad faith actors" opposed to "healthy conversation." Forget guilt by association, this was guilt by notoriety.

After public protests, Twitter restored the congressmen's visibility on the platform, but the underlying issue remains unchanged. Twitter still buries accounts from so-called "bad-faith actors" while remaining opaque about who fits that classification or exactly how its algorithms work.

Twitter's Charm Offensive

After its censorship of Republican congressmen was revealed, Twitter launched a well-publicized "charm offensive" to regain conservatives' trust. Dorsey granted interviews to a handful of conservatives, and the company announced plans to hold a series of meetings with leaders on the right. In one such interview on Fox News Radio, Dorsey used a sleight-of-hand to explain away the controversy. He pointed out that Twitter had shifted to a ranked timeline algorithm two years previously, while not mentioning that the algorithm had been changed to punish "bad-faith actors."[27]

Still, Twitter's charm offensive was successful because it quickly convinced liberal journalists that Twitter was taking conservatives' concerns seriously. "We need to constantly show that we are not adding our own bias, which I fully admit is more left-leaning," Dorsey said on CNN. "And I think it's important to articulate our own bias and to share it with people so that people understand us. But we need to remove our bias from how we act and our policies and our enforcement." Dorsey sounded a similar note in an interview with Recode a few days later, noting that conservatives in the company self-censor to avoid backlash from their liberal colleagues. "I mean, we have a lot of conservative-leaning folks in the company as well, and to be honest, they don't feel safe to express their opinions at the company," Dorsey told Recode. "They do feel silenced by just the general swirl of what they perceive to be the broader percentage of leanings within the company, and I don't think that's fair or right. We should make sure that everyone feels safe to express themselves within the company, no matter where they come from and what their background is."

It's nice that Twitter's CEO was open about his company's left-wing bias when speaking to liberal journalists. But it directly contradicted what his company spokesmen told conservatives in private meetings.

Cuccinelli Delivers a Warning

In one such meeting, two Twitter representatives, both former Republican staffers, assured a room full of conservative politicos that Twitter was a relatively neutral company and that conservatives at

Twitter felt perfectly comfortable expressing their opinions, according to audio I obtained of the meeting, and sources inside the room. Conservatives in the room were skeptical, and some even walked out before the meeting ended. Ken Cuccinelli, then the president of the Senate Conservatives Fund, delivered a fiery rant at Twitter's representatives over the speakerphone. (Full disclosure: I interned for a summer on Cuccinelli's 2013 gubernatorial campaign.) "Twitter is institutionally radically left-wing, and that is never going to change. There are two levels of implementation [of] neutral policy: one is writing neutral policies and one is implementing neutral policies. You can write neutral policies [but] when you have radical left wingers implementing them, then you will get radical left-wing outcomes," said Cuccinelli, who went on to join the Trump administration in 2019. "The solution for us is—and I'll let the Twitter people know— the minute there is a conservative alternative, I'm dropping you guys like a hot rock and I'd like you to take that back to your company. [Senate Conservatives Fund] will encourage all of our members to drop you guys like a hot rock and I'm sure a lot of the other groups in the room will do the same thing," he continued, receiving murmurs of approval from those in attendance. Cuccinelli concluded: "The notion that there isn't a double standard is indefensible."

Twitter's Left-Wing Academics

In fact, instead of guarding against leftist bias at the company, Twitter increased it. On July 30, 2018, Twitter announced that it was launching a task force of academics to fight partisan echo chambers and intolerance. "In the context of growing political polarization, the spread of misinformation, and increases in incivility and intolerance, it is clear that if we are going to effectively evaluate and address some of the most difficult challenges arising on social media, academic researchers and tech companies will need to work together much more closely," said Dr. Rebekah Tromble, the lead professor on the project.[28] As part of the project, Twitter would work with the academics to develop algorithms to combat "intolerant discourse—such as hate speech, racism, and xenophobia," which the company called "inherently threatening to democracy."[29]

We know what happens when left-wing academics are given the power to police "intolerant" speech at institutions. Overt hostility to free speech and due process quickly emerges. Feelings are prioritized over truth. The institution you get resembles the University of California at Berkeley. We're now in the process of seeing what happens when left-wing academics are empowered to draw speech boundaries on social media.

Twitter's Internal Push for More Censorship

In August 2018, Twitter faced a backlash from its own employees for not moving quickly enough to ban conspiracy theorist Alex Jones from the platform, especially as Jones had recently been banned from YouTube and Facebook. "There is no honor in resisting 'outside pressure,' just to pat ourselves on the back for being 'impartial,'" Twitter engineer Marina Zhao wrote in a tweet addressed to her boss, Dorsey. She added: "Twitter does not exist in a vacuum, and it is wrong to ignore the serious real-world harm, and to equate that with political viewpoints."[30]

"I don't agree with everything Twitter does or doesn't do. If we can consistently enforce the policies and terms of service for the platform, that's a good thing. But it doesn't mean we should be satisfied with the policies we have," another Twitter engineer, Mike Cvet, wrote to Dorsey. "It is impossible to promote healthy dialog with bad-faith actors, who regularly produce toxic, dangerous and demonstrably false conspiracy theories; the objective of which is to mislead, radicalize, divide." Cvet said. In a response to Cvet, Dorsey said he also wasn't happy about the company's policies, which he said "need to constantly evolve."[31]

Twitter caved to the internal pressure almost instantly. Twitter vice president Del Harvey sent a company-wide email the very next day announcing plans to accelerate further speech restrictions, citing "a number of conversations with staff about Alex Jones" as the reason. "We're shifting our timeline forward for reviewing the dehumanization policy with staff and will be doing so this week," Harvey assured employees in the internal email. "We're going to move up our timeline around a policy governing off-platform behavior, with a goal of having a recommendation for a path forward for staff review by mid-September or earlier (resource-dependent)." Harvey didn't elaborate on the specific details of the "dehumanization policy" in that email, but it later proved to be (surprise!) a giant step towards restricting free speech on the platform.

■　　■　　■

"Men aren't women." It's a self-evident truth on its own terms. The first entry for "man" in the *Merriam Webster Dictionary* is: "an individual human; *especially*: an adult male human."[32] Its top definition for "woman" is "an adult female person."[33] "Men aren't women" is a truth as obvious as "two plus two equals four." But it's a truth that's becoming increasingly unpopular on the far left, and one that the political and cultural establishment have shown little interest in defending.

Business Insider writer Daniella Greenbaum quit her job after the company bowed to outside pressure and deleted one of her columns. "Scarlett Johansson is the latest target of the social-justice warrior mob. The actress is being chastised for, well, acting," Greenbaum wrote in the offending column. "She has been cast in a movie in which she will play someone different than herself. For this great crime—which seems to essentially define the career path she has chosen—she is being castigated for being insufficiently sensitive to the transgender community."[34] The outrage mobs came for Greenbaum's article and demanded *Business Insider* delete it. Some of Greenbaum's colleagues told management they were uncomfortable with the article. *Business Insider* caved shortly thereafter and pulled the article.[35]

Democratic politicians are making it easier to deny free speech that affirms biological facts by making the recognition of biological facts punishable by law. Congresswoman Ilhan Omar of Minnesota, for instance, wants the government to punish athletic organizations that don't allow biological males to compete against women. The congresswoman called it a "myth" that men who identify as transgender women have a "direct competitive advantage" and urged investigation of "this discriminatory behavior."[36] In May 2019, the House of Representatives passed, with unanimous Democrat support, the Equality Act, which would require schools to include male athletes who identify as transgender girls on female sports teams.[37] Every Democratic presidential candidate polling above one percent endorsed the radical bill.[38]

Social media rulebooks have of course taken up the left's insistence on denying biological realities. Twitter suspended Canadian feminist writer Meghan Murphy in November 2018 for saying that biological men who identify as transgender women aren't real women. Murphy outlined her months-long battle with Twitter on her website, Feminist Current. Once she did, left-wing transgender activists targeted Murphy's account for months, reporting her for alleged hate speech repeatedly.[39]

In August 2018, Twitter dinged Murphy for using male pronouns to refer to a biological male who identifies as a transgender woman. Twitter said Murphy's tweets violated the company's "rules against hateful conduct" and ordered her to delete them to regain access to her account. Murphy complied. Upon regaining access to her account, she called out Twitter for the act of censorship and asked for an explanation: "Hi @Twitter, I'm a journalist. Am I no longer permitted to report facts on your platform?" Twitter retaliated. "I was promptly locked out of my account again, told I had to delete the tweet in question, and suspended for 12 hours. I appealed the suspension, as it seemed clear to me that my tweets were not 'hateful,' but simply stated the truth, but received no response from Twitter," Murphy wrote. The activists continued hounding Twitter to ban Murphy for her linguistic defiance. Three months passed, during which Twitter implemented a new rule that provided the pretense for giving the activists what they wanted.

Twitter announced the change on September 25, 2018, saying it would take action against "dehumanizing" speech in the future. "For the last three months, we have been developing a new policy to address dehumanizing language on Twitter. Language that makes someone less than human can have repercussions off the service, including normalizing serious violence," Twitter announced in a blog post.[40] "With this change, we want to expand our hateful conduct policy to include content that dehumanizes others based on their membership in an identifiable group, even when the material does not include a direct target," the company explained. Twitter vice president Del Harvey explained the tech corporation's reasoning:

> We obviously get reports from people about content that they believe violates our rules that does not. The dehumanizing content and the dehumanizing behavior is one of the areas that really makes up a significant chunk of those reports. We've gotten feedback not just in terms of the research that's out there about potential real-world harms,

we've gotten feedback from the people who use Twitter about this being something they view as deeply problematic. All of those things add together to say we should absolutely be trying to make sure we aren't limiting how we think about our policies to just those that are dealing with whether an individual was specifically referenced.[41]

Harvey's remarks attracted little attention at the time, but they indicated a giant step forward for the pro-censorship crowd: Twitter already banned "hate speech," but that wasn't enough to justify banning the types of tweets and tweeters that leftists wanted banned. Left-wing ideologues wanted people who rejected their narrative to be banned, even though they were fully complying with Twitter's rules. So, Twitter changed the rules.

Twitter didn't reveal just how dramatic the change would be until the following month. In October 2018, Twitter quietly posted this update to its rules: "We prohibit targeting individuals with repeated slurs, tropes or other content that intends to dehumanize, degrade or reinforce negative or harmful stereotypes about a protected category. This includes targeted misgendering or deadnaming of transgender individuals." That is: it was now against Twitter's rules to describe a biological male, who identifies as a transgender woman, as a biological male. It's also against the rules to refer to an individual by their legal name if they've adopted a different name as part of their transgender identity.

Twitter locked Murphy out of her account once again on November 15, citing two tweets she wrote in October. "Men aren't women," Murphy wrote in one tweet. In another, referring to biological males who identify as transgender women, she wrote: "How are transwomen not men? What is the difference between a man and a transwoman?" Twitter once more forced Murphy to delete the tweets to regain access to her account. In an ensuing series of tweets, the feminist writer criticized Twitter's censorship as Orwellian and noted the massive implications at stake: "I'm not allowed to say that men aren't women or ask questions about the notion of transgenderism at all anymore? That a multi-billion dollar company is censoring basic facts and silencing people who ask questions about this dogma is insane." Twitter forced her to delete those tweets as well.

Murphy responded by posting a statement on her website, saying "while Twitter knowingly permits graphic pornography and death threats on the platform (I have reported countless violent threats, the vast majority of which have gone unaddressed), they won't allow me to state very basic facts, such as 'men aren't women.'" Murphy called that glaring contradiction "insane." She added:

This is hardly an abhorrent thing to say, nor should it be considered "hateful" to ask questions about the notion that people can change sex, or ask for explanations about transgender ideology. These are now, like it or not, public debates—debates that are impacting people's lives, as legislation and policy are being imposed based on gender identity ideology (that is, the belief that a male person can "identify" as female or vice versa). That trans activists and their allies may find my questions about what "transgender" means or how a person can literally change sex uncomfortable, as they seem not to be able to respond to them, which I can imagine feels uncomfortably embarrassing, feeling uncomfortable is not a good enough reason to censor and silence people.

Murphy is hardly a conservative, but she recognized that the push for online censorship isn't coming from the right.

There are numerous feminists around the world and unaffiliated members of the general public who see transgender ideology as dangerous (or simply ridiculous), and are critical of the ongoing silencing and smearing of those who challenge it. But one thing that does seem undeniable to me—something that the left should consider carefully, in terms of their own political strategizing—is that while the left seems to have taken to ignoring or refusing to engage with detractors or those who have opinions they disagree with or don't like, the right continues to be interested in and open to engaging. And I think this is a good thing.

Shortly after Murphy posted the statement, Twitter permanently banned her from the platform. The ban signified a seismic shift. When one of the world's most influential platforms makes speaking self-evident truths—like the fact that men aren't women and women aren't men—dependent upon permission, we're well on our way to the dystopian vision George Orwell described in his novel *1984*. Two plus two only equals four until it gets in the way of progressive victories, at which point two plus two may equal three, and you're ignorant and hateful for asserting otherwise.

Twitter suspended Greg Scott, the media director for the Heritage Foundation, in May 2019 for pointing out the unfairness of a biological male competing as a transgender female weightlifter: "If any competitive sport highlights the differences [between] men & women that EVERYONE KNOWS ARE REAL, it is powerlifting."[42] Twitter suspended Scott for violating its "hateful conduct" policies.

"What they force you to do in order to be able to be back on the platform is they essentially, like a fundamentalist religious cult, force you to confess, repent and promise to Jack [Dorsey] that you will be a good Twittizen in the future," Scott told the Daily Caller.[43]

Twitter suspended Ray Blanchard, a well-respected expert on gender dysphoria issues, after he tweeted six positions on transgenderism based on his research in the field:

1. Transsexualism and milder forms of gender dysphoria are types of mental disorder, which may leave the individual with average or even above-average functioning in unrelated areas of life.
2. Sex change surgery is still the best treatment for carefully screened, adult patients, whose gender dysphoria has proven resistant to other forms of treatment.
3. Sex change surgery should not be considered for any patient until that patient has reached the age of 21 years and has lived for at least two years in the desired gender role.
4. Gender dysphoria is not a sexual orientation, but it is virtually always preceded or accompanied by an atypical sexual orientation—in males, either homosexuality (sexual arousal by members of one's own biological sex)...or autogynephilia (sexual arousal at the thought or image of oneself as a female).
5. There are two main types of gender dysphoria in males, one associated with homosexuality and one associated with autogynephilia. Traditionally, the great bulk of female-to-male transsexuals has been homosexual in erotic object choice.
6. The sex of a postoperative transsexual should be analogous to a legal fiction. This legal fiction would apply to some things (e.g., sex designation on a driver's license) but not to others (entering a sports competition as one's adopted sex).

Twitter claimed that Blanchard's first statement violated rules against "hateful conduct" on the platform.[44] Only after a backlash did Twitter backtrack and restore Blanchard's account.

The implications of this new reality extend well beyond feminists concerned about men in dresses invading their spaces. Pope Francis, for example, has consistently rejected the idea that people can choose whether they are a man or a woman. "Today, children are taught this at school: that everyone can choose their own sex. And why do they teach this? Because the books come from those people and institutions who give money. We are living at a time when humankind as the image of God is being annihilated," the Holy Father said in August 2016.[45] "God created man and woman; God created the world like this and we are doing the exact opposite,"[46] he added. In other words, the pope said, men aren't women. Nobody tell Twitter.

■ ■ ■

Twitter's leftist bias explains why the platform is quick to censor right-of-center accounts and slow to punish leftists.

Twitter suspended Nicholas Fondacaro, a writer for the conservative Media Research Center, for example, after he made fun of Don Lemon's annual New Year's Eve routine of getting hammered drunk on national television. Fondacaro credited pressure from conservative media outlets like the Daily Caller for Twitter reinstating his account.[47]

Twitter also permanently suspended a parody account making fun of Democratic presidential candidate Beto O'Rourke in January 2019. The account, called "Beto's Blog," is run by an anonymous user who tweets parody versions of O'Rourke's diary-style blog posts. Twitter said it permanently suspended the account for violating its rules against "impersonation."[48] That excuse is laughable. Twitter is filled with satire and parody accounts targeting everyone across the spectrum—it's one of the things that makes the platform enjoyable. But Twitter agreed with whoever reported "Beto's Blog": the laughs had to go. Once again, Twitter only reversed course after conservative media outlets exposed the company's double-standards.[49]

In another incident, Twitter suspended a user for criticizing Palestinian terrorist organization Hamas, and only reversed its decision after it received an inquiry from the Daily Caller News Foundation, my employer.[50]

Conservative protests aren't always enough, however, to make Twitter reverse its decisions. Twitter banned the Center for Immigration Studies from promoting any tweet that included the words "illegal aliens."[51] Twitter also banned ads for a Christian book that defined marriage as between a man and a woman. In neither case did Twitter reverse its rulings.

Kathleen McKinley

Kathleen McKinley is a conservative blogger and commentator in Houston, Texas. Twitter suspended her in July 2018 for two older tweets that allegedly violated its rules against "hateful conduct." One was a month-old tweet that opposed medically clearing transgender people for military service—a policy position shared by many Republicans and many members of the military. The other tweet, from September 2017, tied "extreme Muslim beliefs" to the practice of honor-killings. Ironically, perhaps, Twitter suspended McKinley one day after a Muslim immigrant in McKinley's hometown was convicted of murdering two people in an honor-killing. McKinley returned to Twitter when her suspension ended but the company has yet to offer her an explanation or an apology for the suspension.

Jesse Kelly

In November 2018, Twitter banned conservative commentator and radio host Jesse Kelly. Unlike the first prominent users Twitter placed in its crosshairs, Kelly is a Marine combat veteran and former Republican congressional candidate. Twitter never told him why he was suspended, which is a clear violation of its own terms of service. I know Jesse. The idea that he's too extreme to participate in public conversation is laughable, as both liberals and conservatives quickly pointed out. Andy Lassner, an executive producer for Ellen Degeneres, slammed Twitter. "I'm as liberal as they come. Jesse is a harmless guy who happens to be funny as hell, not to mention my friend," Lassner tweeted. "If Twitter really banned him, that's just stupid."[52] Republican Senator Ben Sasse of Nebraska, referring specifically to the Jesse Kelly case, agreed, saying that "The trend of de-platforming and shutting down speech is a bad precedent for our free speech society."[53] With criticism mounting, and Republican senators even hinting at Congressional hearings about Twitter's policies, Twitter reinstated Jesse's account, but still refused to explain why it had banned him in the first place.

In an op-ed, Jesse framed Twitter's decision to ban him as part of a larger societal trend and warned that "the American spirit of free speech has been replaced by people who want uncomfortable speech censored. Nowhere is this more apparent than the social media world." Kelly noted the massive influence that Big Tech has accumulated in our lives and our politics: "As I have said before, social media is not a small thing. It is no longer three nerds with pocket protectors huddled in their dorm rooms dreaming about a day when a woman acknowledges their existence. Social media has surpassed the telephone. It is the means of networking and communicating with others: 2.5 billion people use Facebook and Twitter. That is not a fringe thing that is going away. It has now become the way humans interact with each other. It is completely run by Silicon Valley leftists who know the power they hold. And they are using that power."[54]

"Learn to Code"

Any doubts about the influence liberal journalists exercise over Twitter were eliminated by the "learn to code" fiasco. When coal miners lose their jobs, journalists often write about creative destruction and the evolving modern economy. *They'll just have to learn how to code* is a common attitude. But of course when journalists lose their jobs, journalists write about the free press becoming endangered and the need for protective legislation. After Vice, HuffPost, and BuzzFeed News laid off dozens of journalists in January 2019, some Internet trolls mocked them with the phrase "Learn to Code." In response, journalists lobbied Twitter to penalize people who tweeted the phrase at them. Twitter obliged, essentially declaring the joke off-limits on the platform. After critics pointed out the absurdity of Twitter suspending people for tweeting "learn to code," the company claimed it was only penalizing users who took part in a "targeted harassment campaign against specific individuals—a policy that's long been against the Twitter Rules."[55] That clearly wasn't true. Twitter suspended Daily Caller editor in chief Geoffrey Ingersoll for tweeting "Learn to code" at the *Daily Show*, a Comedy Central show that wasn't a target of any organized campaign.[56]

Dana Loesch

Liberal Twitter users regularly launch vile and disgusting attacks on former National Rifle Association spokeswoman Dana Loesch, without getting dinged for rule violations. "You feckless cunt." "Stupid cunt." "You, lady, are a stupid fucking cunt. Rot in hell." "Whose cock did you suck Dana?" "Typical gun-toting racist bitch." Those are all real tweets that have been directed at Loesch—and they're only a tiny sample of the abuse she regularly experiences on Twitter every day. But Twitter doesn't care.

Dana and her husband, Chris Loesch, once reported a liberal Twitter user who said that if the couple's children "need to be murdered" for Dana to change her mind about gun control, then "I guess that's what needs to happen." Twitter reviewed their report and returned a verdict: the tweet was fine. "We have reviewed your report carefully and found that there was no violation of the Twitter Rules against abusive behavior," Twitter wrote in an email to Chris.[57] It was only after the Loesches went public with Twitter's response and conservative media put Twitter on blast (notice a trend?) that Twitter announced it had "re-reviewed" Chris's report. "We have re-reviewed the account you reported and have locked it because we found it to be in violation of the Twitter Rules," the company wrote in an email to Chris. Twitter also noted that the user would be allowed to reenter the platform as soon as he deleted his tweet about murdering Dana's kids.[58] (The same condition that it placed on Meghan Murphy's tweets about biological sex.)

The incident occurred in October 2018, a full year after Twitter made a public show about protecting its users. But Twitter doesn't actually care about protecting all of its users. The rules do not exist to be neutrally enforced; the rules exist to give Twitter a basis for caving whenever the left wants a tweet deleted or a tweeter blocked. In late 2016, Dana received death threats on Twitter that were serious and detailed enough that the couple contacted the police. The police began an investigation, but Twitter got in the way. Documents I obtained show that law enforcement officials reported that they had "completed and submitted grand jury subpoenas to Twitter [but] Twitter declined to acknowledge the subpoena and release any information despite our [county] grand jury issuing the order."

Twitter doesn't take threats against conservatives seriously, and that's especially the case for conservative women. Just ask Meghan McCain.

Meghan McCain

Meghan McCain, a host on *The View* and the daughter of the late senator and Vietnam hero John McCain, has been a regular target of hate and bile on Twitter. But Twitter, which aggressively cracked down on conservatives who tweeted "learn to code," was curiously slow to respond to the hatred directed at McCain. In the days after John McCain's funeral, for example, a Twitter user posted a doctored photo showing a gun pointed at Meghan as she approached her father's casket. "*America, this ones for you,*" the photo's caption read. The tweet remained on the platform for more than twelve hours, despite dozens of conservatives reporting it to Twitter and asking the site to take it down. Only after Meghan's husband, Ben Domenech, tweeted at Dorsey directly did Twitter remove the tweet. "Hey @jack, this has been up for half a day. It has been reported 100+ times. No response. Tell me why this is cool by you," Domenech wrote.[59] Once again, Twitter only took action because a concerted effort from conservatives criticizing both the company and Dorsey personally made deleting the offending post the better public relations option.

Dorsey was asked about Twitter's hesitance to remove the death threats against McCain when he testified before Congress on September 5, 2018. "That was unacceptable," Dorsey replied. When the committee asked if he had apologized to the McCain family, Dorsey said, "I haven't personally, but I will."[60] Days passed without an apology, then weeks, and then months. Still, no apology arrived. Perhaps Dorsey forgot about the promise he made *under oath*? Perhaps, but unlikely. Domenech published a scathing article in November 2018, castigating Dorsey for his broken promise. "Jack Dorsey has never contacted my wife or me to apologize," Domenech wrote in an article titled, "Twitter CEO Jack Dorsey Lied Under Oath To Congress. Shouldn't That Matter?"[61] You might assume that after Domenech's public reminder of the broken promise, Dorsey would have leapt into action, but that wasn't the case. Yet more days passed without an apology, then weeks, and then months. Domenech told me that Dorsey finally called at the end of January 2019—nearly five months after he promised Congress that he would. The incident was a microcosm of Dorsey's entire playbook when confronted about his company's left-wing bias: pay lip service to the problem and then do as little as possible to actually address it.

Twitter's Journalists

Twitter long billed itself as a passive platform, but in June 2018, Twitter announced it would emphasize breaking news, with personalized news feeds for each user.[62] Twitter product vice president Keith Coleman explained to *Bloomberg News* that Dorsey "often says we want Twitter to be the little bird on your shoulder that tells you what you need to know, when you need to know it. When something important happens on Twitter, we want Twitter to tap you on the shoulder and say 'hey, this is going on and we want you to check it out.'" Social media is already personalized by the consumer: people choose what to read. Twitter seeks to "personalize" it on the producer end: it will tell you what to read. Telling consumers what to read, however, is exercising news judgment—which is the job of journalists. The company's own postings make it clear that Twitter is now in the journalism business, whether it acknowledges it or not.

"We're looking for an experienced, innovative and detail-oriented reporter, expert in social media and passionate about journalism, to fill out the team," one December 2018 job posting read.[63] The opening was for a position on Twitter's "breaking news team." The job posting explained that "Twitter is where news is most often first reported, and a single Tweet often drives the news agendas of the world's largest media companies. The breaking news team will be part of an experimental initiative to detect, verify and explain the biggest stories breaking on Twitter in real time." It informed applicants that as "a member of the Curation team, you will be based in San Francisco, and report to the deputy breaking news lead. In this role, you will be responsible for monitoring and verifying news alerts, quickly and accurately summarizing and updating them, and sourcing Tweets that accurately explain and contextualize what is happening in real time." Journalism. That's called journalism.

The process described in that job post is essentially the same process that breaking news teams at CNN and Fox News go through. The difference is that CNN and Fox News acknowledge that they're media companies. Twitter doesn't but is moving into that role in order to keep users on the platform longer. As a bonus it will further control what users see on the platform.

Twitter is becoming just another liberal news company—and the early results have been atrocious. In January 2019, Twitter helped amplify a vicious smear against a group of students from Covington Catholic High School in Lexington, Kentucky. The boys, some of whom wore MAGA hats, were in Washington, D.C., for the 2019 March for Life. The way the story was told, the group of boys swarmed an elderly Native American man, Nathan Phillips, and racially harassed him as he tried to walk away from the Indigenous People's March the same day. A selectively edited clip showed Phillips beating his drum in front of a boisterous crowd of boys, and it was alleged that the boys had racially harassed the old man. Phillips gave a teary-eyed monologue about the sad incident and what it meant for America. Journalists fawned. There was just one problem: none of it was true. Had any journalists watched the full video before sending social media mobs at high school students, they would have seen that Phillips was lying.

"Far from engaging in racially motivated harassment, the group of mostly white, MAGA-hat-wearing male teenagers remained relatively calm and restrained despite being subjected to incessant racist, homophobic, and bigoted verbal abuse by members of the bizarre religious sect Black Hebrew Israelites, who were lurking nearby. The BHI has existed since the late nineteenth century and is best described as a black nationalist cult movement; its members believe they are descendants of the ancient Israelites, and often express condemnation of white people, Christians, and gays. D.C.-area Black Hebrews are known to spout particularly vile bigotry," *Reason* magazine's Robby Soave wrote in a thorough debunking of the media's smear job. "Phillips put himself between the teens and the black nationalists, chanting and drumming as he marched straight into the middle of the group of young people. What followed was several minutes of confusion: The teens couldn't quite decide whether Phillips was on their side or not, but tentatively joined in his chanting. It's not at all clear this was intended as an act of mockery rather than solidarity." Soave called it "as misguided a rush to judgment as the [famously false] *Rolling Stone* story" about an alleged gang rape at the University of Virginia. (He was one of the few journalists to question that egregious hoax as well.)

Twitter promoted the misleading narrative about the Covington High School students to its millions of users in its curated "Moments" feature, stating "A diocese in Kentucky is investigating after a video showed students from Covington Catholic High School taunting Omaha elder and Vietnam veteran Nathan Phillips at a rally in Washington. Many of the students were wearing 'Make America Great Again' hats."[64]

The story was then off and running on Twitter, which added a *New York Times* tweet that read: "Video showing a group of high school boys, many wearing 'Make America Great Again' gear, surrounding and jeering a Native American elder at the Indigenous Peoples March in Washington, is drawing widespread condemnation." Twitter also included a tweet from CNN commentator Ana Navarro, which read: "Native-American elder taunted by racist MAGA-hat wearing teens, speaks and cries for America, the country he defended and sacrificed and wore the uniform for. It is people like Nathan Phillips who make America great."

Not only did Twitter direct hate against high school students who never asked to be famous, they then stood by as Kathy Griffin and other prominent liberals urged their followers to publicly identify the boys in the video so they could be more thoroughly shamed. Left-wingers soon posted online the names, addresses, emails, and phone numbers of Covington students and their families. Their students' and families' voicemail and inboxes were flooded with hate and threats of violence. I reported Griffin to Twitter—she was clearly violating Twitter's terms of service, and Twitter did nothing.

The establishment liberal media that Big Tech wants to elevate as "authoritative" sources were culpable in the smearing of these high school students. The people who exposed the truth were the sort of reporters or "citizen journalists" that Big Tech wants to marginalize. For Big Tech, the issue isn't about free speech, or true investigative reporting, or telling the truth—it's about advancing an agenda.

What Trends, What Doesn't, and Why?

Twitter's trending topics section has tremendous influence over its users. It directs the attention of tens of millions of people towards a handful of topics. When Twitter users click a trending topic, they'll see tweets on the subject from people they follow intermixed with the top results. Tweeting about trending topics makes a user's tweets more likely to be seen, and it also means that whoever decides what's trending has an enormous amount of power over the national discussion. In the early days of Twitter, what trended was determined by how rapidly and often a hashtag was tweeted.

Twitter eventually expanded its trending section to include both hashtags and topics, which is part of transformed Twitter into a news aggregator: its Moments Trending Topics sections are where users track national conversations. So, who decides what trends and what doesn't? Twitter's liberal journalists—the ones who write news articles without bylines. That gives them enormous power over the national discussion.

When the Covington faux scandal exploded, Twitter fanned the flames. But when Democrats drew heat for backing late-term abortions and even infanticide, it wasn't a Twitter trending topic. That's not a coincidence. Twitter doesn't just follow or reflect national conversations; it tries to direct them.

The political balance of power on Twitter has shifted substantially since Trump was elected. Many of the president's biggest right-wing fans on Twitter are gone from the platform. And given that Twitter has become just another arm of the liberal establishment media, it seems unlikely they'll be back. Twitter is no longer a platform of free-for-all conversations; instead, it has become part of the great liberal media echo chamber.

CHAPTER SIX

Purging Pro-Lifers

Renowned Princeton professor Robert P. George is known to walk his undergraduate students through a thought experiment when discussing America's history of racial injustice, in order to demonstrate the moral courage that abolitionists possessed. Had you been white and living in the slave-holding old South, George asks his students, how many of you would have been abolitionists? Invariably, every hand in the class shoots up. But the lopsided outcome of the vote, George asserts, is the product of hindsight-bias and wishful thinking. "Of course, it is complete nonsense. Only the tiniest fraction of them, or of any of us, would have spoken up against slavery or lifted a finger to free the slaves. Most of them—and us—would simply have gone along. Many would have supported the slave system and, if it was in their interest, participated in it as buyers and owners or sellers of slaves," George once explained, when asked about the exercise.[1] He continued:

So I respond to the students' assurances that they would have been vocal opponents of slavery by saying that I will credit their claims if they can show me evidence of the following: that in leading their lives today they have embraced causes that are unpopular among their peers and stood up for the rights of victims of injustice whose very humanity is denied, and where they have done so knowing (1) that it would make THEM unpopular with their peers, (2) that they would be loathed and ridiculed by wealthy, powerful, and influential individuals and institutions in our society; (3) that it would cost them friendships and cause them to be abandoned and even denounced by many of their friends, (4) that they would be called nasty names, and (5) that they would possibly even be denied valuable educational and professional opportunities as a result of their moral witness.In short, my challenge to them is to show me where they have at significant risk to themselves and their futures stood up for a cause that is unpopular in elite sectors of our culture today.

The moral courage that it took to be an abolitionist in the antebellum South is the moral courage required to be a pro-life activist in America today. If you run through George's five points again, you will easily see how they apply to pro-lifers. In America's dominant media, corporate, and academic institutions, defending an unborn child's right to life marks you as a "gender-traitor" if you're a woman and as a "misogynist" if you're a man. In many cases, you can expect to pay a price, in personal vilification if nothing else, and that's especially true in the world of Big Tech. Big Tech is unwavering in its support for Planned Parenthood and other abortion-advocacy groups.

The Radicals

Abortion activists, liberal journalists, and Big Tech frame the abortion debate in highly misleading ways. Mainstream media coverage consistently portrays the pro-life movement as one dominated by dangerous extremists, while promoting radical, far-left organizations like Planned Parenthood and NARAL Pro-Choice America as mere health care providers.

In truth, Planned Parenthood and its allies who support abortion on demand are far outside the political mainstream—and the numbers prove it. A June 2018 Gallup poll found that 60 percent of America adults "think abortion should generally be legal in the first three months of pregnancy. However, support drops by about half, to 28 percent, for abortions conducted in the second three months, and by half again, to 13 percent, in the final three months."[2] Those findings were consistent with Gallup's last twenty years of polling on the subject, a senior Gallup editor noted. Polling from other reputable outlets like Marist also show that a sizable majority of Americans support significant restrictions on abortion.[3] Legality aside, most Americans, in twenty years of Gallup polling, consistently say abortion is morally wrong.[4]

Yet, in January 2019, when New York's legislature approved a bill allowing abortion up until birth, Planned Parenthood tweeted a video of pro-abortion activists erupting in cheers—cheering something that most Americans think is morally wrong and that is supported by only 13 percent of American adults. Planned Parenthood goes beyond extremism to ghoulishness with its PR campaigns like #ShoutYourAbortion, encouraging women to take pride in having an abortion.

Discussing the realities of third-trimester abortions—at ten weeks, you can pick up the unborn baby's heartbeat on an ultrasound;[5] at twenty-two weeks a baby will likely survive premature birth[6]—and having conversations about the morality of later term abortions, are the abortion lobby's nightmare, so wherever possible, they try silencing opposing views. Within the Democrat Party, support for unlimited abortion on demand has become a litmus test that no liberal politician can afford to fail.

In 2017 and 2018, Planned Parenthood's political arm gave $6.9 million to election committees,[7] spent another $2.5 million lobbying, and wrote checks for an additional $3.8 million to support Democratic candidates, $4.1 million to oppose Republican candidates, and nearly $200,000 to undercut Democratic primary candidates who weren't pro-abortion enough.[8]

Through its financial clout, the abortion lobby has frog-marched the Democratic Party to abortion extremism. From 1996 through 2004, the Democratic Party platform repeated variations of the idea that abortion "should be safe, legal, and rare." But when Barack Obama was nominated in 2008, the party dropped "rare" from the equation, and the term hasn't returned in any of its platforms since then.[9] The Democrats' platform in 2016 was the first major party platform to explicitly call for the repeal of the Hyde Amendment, which prohibits the use of federal funds for abortion except in cases of rape, incest, or to save the life of the mother.[10] Shortly after launching his 2020 presidential campaign, former Vice President Joe Biden felt compelled to abandon his decades-long support for the Hyde Amendment.

As extremists often do, Planned Parenthood has made common cause with other extreme organizations. It was one of a few left-wing groups that proudly stood by the Women's March after that organization was rocked by a series of scandals exposing antisemitism at its highest levels. Women's March leaders had publicly declared solidarity with Nation of Islam leader Louis Farrakhan, a notorious antisemite who has praised Hitler and described Jews as "termites" and

"Satanic."[11] One Women's March leader, Tamika Mallory, initially defended Farrakhan by implying that religious leaders are supposed to consider Jews their enemies.[12] The group was later revealed to have worked closely with Nation of Islam members, including using them for security,[13] and Women's March leaders were repeatedly quoted making antisemitic remarks.[14] Yet as left-wing groups like the SPLC quietly distanced themselves from the scandal-ridden group, Planned Parenthood stood with Women's March.[15] Even the Democratic National Committee cut ties with March because it was so extreme. But not Planned Parenthood. The abortion advocate proudly supported the group and co-sponsored its events around the country.

■   ■   ■

As Planned Parenthood is silencing dissent from its agenda within the Democratic Party, the pro-abortion lobby and its supporters are trying to do the same in our culture at large. Rossalyn Warren, a political activist and feminist, published an op-ed in the *New York Times* accusing Facebook of allowing "fake news" on its platform in October 2017. Facebook's crime? Not censoring pro-life news websites as much as she would like.[16] Warren wrote:

> LifeNews, which has just under one million followers on Facebook, is one of several large anti-abortion sites that can command hundreds of thousands of views on a single post. These sites produce vast amounts of misinformation; the Facebook page for the organization Live Action, for instance, has two million Facebook followers and posts videos claiming there's a correlation between abortion and breast cancer. And their stories often generate more engagement than the content produced by mainstream

news organizations, said Sharon Kann, the program director for abortion rights and reproductive health at Media Matters, a watchdog group. People on Facebook engage with anti-abortion content more than abortion-rights content at a "disproportionate rate," she said, which, as a result of the company's algorithms, means more people see it.[17]

In other words, an op-ed piece in the *New York Times* argued that Facebook should rig its algorithms against pro-life content, apparently as news that's not fit to print. Something similar happened at *The Atlantic*, after it ran a piece by *National Review* staff writer Alexandra DeSanctis (who is an unfailingly courageous voice for the unborn) titled, "Democrats Overplay Their Hand on Abortion." Feminist author Jessica Valenti slammed *The Atlantic* for publishing DeSanctis' article; DeSanctis, she said, failed to consider "the incredibly complex moral decision to extend or withdraw care to a preemie"—that is whether to let newborn babies die, if they have health problems.[18] In short, the pro-abortion radicals want to shut down pro-life voices and shift the debate so that even defending the right to life of *newborn infants* is controversial.

And they're not only making the case in print; they're making it on the streets. Pro-abortion activists have taken to angrily protesting outside pro-life women's health clinics,[19] and harassing pro-life women who quietly pray the rosary outside of abortion clinics. In Pennsylvania, Democratic state representative Brian Sims recorded himself accosting an elderly woman for praying outside of a Philadelphia Planned Parenthood clinic. In another video Sims posted to social media, he offered a $100 reward for the identities of three teen girls praying outside the abortion clinic.[20] If you support infanticide, if you believe in silencing popular pro-life voices, if you harass women and teen girls for peacefully praying—and brag about it—then you're clearly on the wrong side, the extremist side. And that's the side Big Tech is on.

The Women Who Won't Be Silenced

Lila Rose founded the pro-life advocacy group Live Action while still in high school. Her original goal was to educate her peers about the realities of abortion and to affirm human dignity at every stage of life. She continued that mission through college, and today Live Action has the largest digital following of any pro-life organization in America. Between Rose's accounts and Live Action's accounts, they have more than 200,000 followers on Twitter and three million followers on Facebook. But, as Rose told me in an interview, her success has been in spite of Big Tech's efforts to bury her message:

> Twitter has now for over two years completely banned our ad accounts, so both Live Action's account and my own account. The reason that they said we're banned from doing any type of advertising on their platform is we violate their hate and sensitive topics policy. When we've gone back and forth with the reps for Twitter's policy team, we're told that in order for us to advertise on Twitter, we would have to delete all content from our website as well as our Twitter feed that talks about what abortion is, that criticizes Planned Parenthood, that shows images of an ultrasound in the context of the pro-life fight.

Live Action was subjected to "extreme demands from Twitter management for us to be able to advertise on their platform and meanwhile Planned Parenthood and other pro-abortion groups continue to advertise with no issues," Rose added.

Twitter even ordered Rose to delete a tweet quoting Thomas Jefferson. The offending tweet included an ultrasound of an unborn child and contained the caption: "'The care of human life and happiness, and not their destruction, is the first and only object of good government.' —Thomas Jefferson." That was the entire "offensive" tweet—a picture of an ultrasound and a quote from a founding father calling for the "care of human life and happiness." No honest person would consider that Jefferson quote offensive, but once it was presented within the context of a pro-life argument, it crossed the line for the ideologues at Twitter. To be sure, the "problem" was not the content of the quote that Lila Rose tweeted; the problem was the fact that *Lila Rose* had tweeted it. Apparently, history is off-limits to people who profess the humanity of unborn children.

Digital advertisements help companies and organizations reach people who otherwise wouldn't know about their products, missions, or messages; and pro-abortion activists are intent on keeping that realm for themselves.

"I was very excited about the rise of new media in the last ten-plus years, because now the traditional media are not the gatekeepers of ideas that they have been with institutions like the school system, which is increasingly leftist, and [in] academia, but if the tech companies also become gatekeepers of ideas, while at the same time doing it in a secretive way, then we have got a huge problem on our hands," Rose told me. "Information is what changes hearts and minds. If people don't have access to those revolutionary ideas, then they are going to be stuck in one silo of thought that, unfortunately, is a very vicious, pro-abortion, anti-life worldview. And that's exactly what we're fighting against," she added. "I'm very concerned about these [pro-censorship] trends by these platforms."

"There's no question that Twitter has chosen a pro-abortion ideology, even though they won't admit that publicly," Rose told me. "Jack Dorsey—in front of a congressional committee—said 'we don't discriminate based on political viewpoint,' and yet discriminating based on viewpoint is exactly what they're doing right now in disallowing Live Action from doing any advertising and continuing to allow pro-abortion groups [to advertise without restrictions]."

"As Live Action has grown and become more formidable and expanded the reach of our platform, we've experienced growing hostility from social media companies," Rose said. That hostility seems to be reflected in the social media companies' changing algorithms, as every change has led to lower levels of engagement with Live Action media.

The algorithms are secret, but sometimes the suppression is obvious. In January 2019, YouTube deleted a Live Action video about Planned Parenthood. Curiously, the allegedly offensive video had been available on the website for nearly eight years without issue, before it was suddenly removed. YouTube warned Live Action that its allegedly inappropriate content merited a "strike" and that additional "strikes" could result in the permanent termination of their account. Live Action appealed the decision, but YouTube promptly rejected it. It was only after Rose publicized the deletion and the ensuing denial of Live Action's appeal that YouTube reinstated the video and reversed the strike against Live Action's account. The reality of abortion is unnerving—it's natural to be outraged by the slaughter of a human baby—and something you won't learn from establishment media sources whose journalists accept awards at Planned Parenthood banquets.[21] So, it's not surprising that pro-life videos draws eyeballs on YouTube. In December 2018, a writer for the left-wing website *Slate* wrote a hysterical article complaining that YouTube wasn't (yet) banning pro-life results from its top search results for "abortion."[22] If Big Tech doesn't run interference, the pro-life argument will always outperform the pro-abortion argument. And that is exactly why Big Tech insists on getting in the way.

Immediately following *Slate*'s article, YouTube manipulated the results for "abortion" searches to replace pro-life videos on the front page with pro-abortion content.[23] Internal documents leaked in January 2019 show that after the *Slate* reporter emailed YouTube about the video, the term "abortion" was reportedly added to a list of "controversial" terms, which one engineer described as a "blacklist."[24] Search results for all of the terms on the list automatically prioritize videos YouTube deemed "authoritative." In other words, it prioritized videos from YouTube-approved news outlets. YouTube will allow videos from EWTN (a Catholic network founded by nuns) through the filter, so it can claim it isn't biased, while burying most pro-life voices, including the pro-life videos identified by the *Slate* reporter. YouTube eventually claimed that the pro-life videos in question were problematic because they "contained misinformation alongside graphic images" and thus had to be pushed off of the front page.[25] Both parts of that explanation are misleading. The videos in question were accurate—they only told plain truths the pro-abortion lobby doesn't like—and only one of the videos could objectively be described as "graphic," and it was no more graphic than many other YouTube videos.[26] YouTube, for instance, has graphic heart surgery videos. The difference is that abortion-related images aren't just graphic, they're disturbing; they reveal the true nature of abortion—that it involves the murder of an unborn baby. You can't see a human arm in an abortionist's tray and come away with any other conclusion. That's the difference between tech companies' disparate treatment of images of heart surgery and images of abortion: the latter is a reality that liberal media companies won't show you. As British politician and Christian evangelist William Wilberforce told the

House of Commons in one of his speeches against the slave trade: "You may choose to look the other way, but you can never say again that you did not know."[27] Intentionally hiding the truth about a moral evil from the public, as YouTube chooses to do, is a shameful display of moral cowardice.

Big Tech vs. Susan B. Anthony

The Susan B. Anthony List (SBA List) is a national network of more than 700,000 pro-life Americans.[28] The group's president, Marjorie Dannenfelser, launched the group as a way to help pro-life women win elected office.[29] Facebook deleted multiple ads from the Susan B. Anthony List, just before the 2018 midterm elections. One of the ads contrasted Democratic Senate candidate Phil Bredesen's support for taxpayer-funded abortion with Republican candidate Marsha Blackburn's support for ending partial-birth abortion.

"SBA List has faced repeated censorship over the last few weeks and now our ad supporting Marsha Blackburn has been disapproved, even after more than 90,000 had viewed it. Facebook must immediately stop its censorship of pro-life speech. All the information presented in our ads has been factual, if surprising to those unwilling to face the reality of pro-abortion extremism. Facebook is censoring the truth and political free speech," SBA List President Marjorie Dannenfelser said at the time.[30]

Facebook blocked another two SBA List ads as well. The videos shared the stories of two babies, Charlotte and Micah, who survived premature births. Facebook dinged them for violating policies against "sensational" content.[31] As far as pro-life ads go, they were pretty boilerplate, but that was still too extreme for Facebook's speech police. Only after intense public pressure from conservative media did Facebook reverse course and apologize for the "mistake."

In October 2017, Twitter blocked an SBA List advertisement from running because it contained the words "killing babies."[32] As Dannenfelser recounted: "No advertiser is permitted to use the phrase 'killing babies'. That's what Twitter told us when they censored one of our videos."[33] The objective truth about abortion is it kills an unborn baby. Twitter would rather people didn't see that truth.

"Some organizations seem determined to censor the pro-life message. The people who run these mega-companies manipulate the national discussion to conform to their political leanings and use their platforms to steer public opinion in their favor," Arizona Republican congressman Andy Biggs warned in a January 2018 op-ed.[34] It's only gotten worse since then.

Facebook blocked producers of the movie *Roe v. Wade* from buying ads promoting their film.[35] The movie was notable for taking a pro-life and anti-Planned Parenthood perspective.[36] Once again, Planned Parenthood's allies came to the rescue. They've done so repeatedly.

In 2017, Twitter blocked a Marsha Blackburn campaign video, hiding "behind the farcical argument that her pro-life rhetoric was 'inflammatory' and that it could 'evoke a strong negative reaction,'" noted the *Washington Examiner*'s Becket Adams.[37] While at the same time, Twitter allowed ReproAction, a pro-abortion political group, to buy inflammatory ads urging Twitter to bar Blackburn from buying pro-life ads.[38] The Texas-based pro-life group Human Coalition has repeatedly seen its content censored by tech companies. On February 21, 2018, Twitter removed three pro-life Human Coalition ads for allegedly violating company policies against "inappropriate content" and placed the group's advertising privileges "under review." Twitter informed Human Coalition the group would receive an email "when the review is complete." That email came March 22: Human Coalition's account was suspended from running ads—any ads—on Twitter. Human Coalition appealed but to no avail. Five days later, I reached out to Twitter's press team and asked three questions:

- What, specifically, was the policy violation that led to this action?
- It's my understanding that Planned Parenthood (@PPFA) is eligible to run advertisements. Is that the case?
- If so, what is the difference between @PPFA and @HumanCoalition?

Two hours after my email to Twitter, Human Coalition received a surprise update: Twitter reversed their suspension and cleared them to run ads again. Twitter assured me that the timing was a coincidence. Anyone familiar with Big Tech's handling of censorship knows better.

Among Facebook's fact-checking partners (more on that in the next chapter) is a left-wing outlet called Health Feedback. To give you an example of how this bias manifests in fact checks, consider what happened when Health Feedback evaluated a Live Action video that asserted, "abortion is never medically necessary."[39] To "fact check" that claim, the left-wing fact checker turned to—who else?—left-wing abortionists. Among them: Dr. Jennifer Gunter, an abortionist who openly advocates for pro-lifers to be censored online, and who had attacked Lila Rose as "ignorant and evil."[40] An investigation by the International Fact-Checking Network (yes, that's a real thing) found that Health Feedback's fact check of Live Action for Facebook "fell short" of the IFCN's standards.[41]

Big Tech's Coziness with the Abortion Lobby

Big Tech's hostility to pro-lifers isn't terribly surprising in light of how close it is with Planned Parenthood and the rest of the abortion industry. Google employees openly support and fundraise for Planned Parenthood inside the company. "Employees at Google organized to raise funds for Planned Parenthood and launched internal initiatives under the Tech Stands with Planned Parenthood campaign," Planned Parenthood's 2016-2017 annual report noted. "Many other tech supporters have continued to show their support through local partnerships with Planned Parenthood affiliates, hosting matching campaigns, and more," the report said.[42]

Facebook's Sheryl Sandberg is a longtime donor to Planned Parenthood and donated one million dollars to the abortion giant in early 2017.[43] In June 2019, Sandberg announced she was making another million-dollar donation—this time to Planned Parenthood's political arm. Sandberg cited the recent wave of state-level pro-life bills as her reason for the donation. "I think this is a very urgent moment where the rights and the choices and the basic health of the most vulnerable women—the women who have been marginalized, often women of color—are at stake," the Facebook executive told the HuffPost. "And so all of us have to do our part to fight these draconian laws."[44] Of course Sandberg is not alone at Facebook. Mark Zuckerberg and his wife donated $992 million in Facebook shares to the Silicon Valley Community Foundation, a liberal donor network that doles out millions of dollars to Planned Parenthood and its affiliates every year.[45]

Lila Rose told me that because Sandberg is "publicly aligning herself with the biggest pro-abortion corporation in the country, a scandal-ridden organization that is extreme in its political lobbying to expand abortion in this country…it's no wonder that confidence in the words of these platforms is low."

To Big Tech, Planned Parenthood and abortion are sacrosanct and should be promoted and protected at all costs. But when it comes to pro-life groups striving to inform people about the reality of abortion and about the moral case for defending human life, Big Tech thinks they need to be silenced.

CHAPTER SEVEN

Speech Police

Progressive activists are working overtime to scare companies from advertising on conservative television shows and websites. They turn every advertisement that airs on a remotely conservative program into a political statement, regardless of the advertising companies' intent. If a company advertises on Fox News at 8:15 p.m. on a week-night, it's no longer treated for what it is: a simple attempt to sell a product to the massive audience that tunes into Tucker Carlson. Instead, progressive activists contort a company's decision to market its product into de facto endorsements of everything that a host says on a show. It's a ridiculous standard that is applied only to conservative media.

In April 2018, Internet sleuths dug up and published a slew of homophobic posts that left-wing pundit Joy Reid wrote on her blog before she joined MSNBC. Reid responded to the story by lying, claiming her social media accounts had been hacked. But the Internet sleuths kept finding more offensive posts published under Reid's name and archives documenting that the blog posts weren't the result of hackers. If this controversy had involved a conservative Fox News host, there's no doubt that left-wing activists would have whipped up an outrage mob, demanded her resignation, and launched a pressure campaign against all of her advertisers. Every advertiser on Reid's show would have been forced to answer some version of the following question: "Joy Reid has a history of anti-gay posts and attempted to lie her way out of it. Are you going to continue advertising on her show?" Once one company said "no," others would follow. Liberal journalists would publish running lists of companies boycotting her show and companies that remained and that "were on the wrong side of history." And the campaign would end with Reid getting fired.

But none of that happened, because Joy Reid is part of the left-wing media establishment. To be clear, I don't want Reid to lose her job, but the fact that left-wing activists showed no interest in applying the same standards to her as they would a Fox News host speaks volumes. They're unprincipled political hitmen, whose job is to silence the opposition. It's a cynical and dishonest strategy. But it's effective.

After the 2016 election, the left-wing activist group Sleeping Giants launched a campaign to convince companies to stop advertising on the pro-Trump website Breitbart News. In the first two months of 2017, *90 percent* of Breitbart's advertisers capitulated to the left-wing pressure and blacklisted the site.[1] Sleeping Giants did not let up. The group urged universities and other institutions to boycott a hedge fund because its chairman, Robert Mercer, was a primary investor in Breitbart. It didn't take long before Mercer resigned from the hedge fund.[2]

The founder of Sleeping Giants, Matt Rivitz, remained anonymous until July 2018 when I identified him after an extensive investigation.[3] (As it turned out, Rivitz was working as an advertising executive.) More than three years after Trump took office, Sleeping

Giants's boycott campaign continues to slowly pick off Breitbart's remaining advertisers.

Liberal activists use similar tactics with Big Tech companies when it comes to policing speech. The activists have significant leverage, because Facebook, Twitter, and Google (and therefore YouTube), rely heavily on ads for revenue, and, of course, Big Tech is largely sympathetic to the activists' goal of making corporations responsible for limiting free speech. That means, in practice, that companies are expected to guarantee that they won't finance, through advertising, speech that liberals deem unacceptable. The tactic isn't new, but it's rapidly gaining steam. The left-wing group Media Matters (founded by liberal hatchet man David Brock[4]) has waged advertisement boycotts against Fox News for years, and other leftist groups have waged similar campaigns against popular conservatives online. Time and again, corporations have bent the knee to left-wing activists.

The SPLC

Groups like the Southern Poverty Law Center often assist these campaigns. The SPLC is a once-respected discrimination watchdog that has long since devolved into a smear-mongering fundraising mill.[5] The SPLC routinely labels mainstream conservatives as "extremists" and Christian organizations as "hate groups."

The SPLC doesn't even pretend to police the left: a spokeswoman for the company admitted to *Politico* in a June 2017 story that the SPLC is "focused, whether people like it or not, on the radical right."[6] And liberal millionaires throw their money at the SPLC for that very reason—to prove how progressive they are. It's laughable that Big Tech uses the SPLC as a referee: the SPLC makes no pretense of being impartial, and its "facts" are often wrong. In November 2016, the

SPLC published a list of "anti-Muslim" extremists that was so wildly inaccurate that it would have been funny if Big Tech, the liberal media, and Democratic lawmakers didn't promote the SPLC as an authoritative voice. The list of alleged-Islamophobes included Ayaan Hirsi Ali, a celebrated human rights activist who survived the barbaric practice of female genital mutilation and works incessantly to save other Muslim girls from suffering a similar fate. Nobody familiar with Hirsi Ali could argue that she is anything other than a hero and a champion of women's rights. And yet, the SPLC casually included her on a list of what the SPLC alleged were extremists linked to inciting anti-Muslim violence. "This misinformation and hateful rhetoric have consequences. When huge numbers of Americans believe that a majority of Muslims are terrorists or terrorist sympathizers, it can hardly be a surprise that some percentage of them engage in hate crime attacks," the SPLC guide warned. "After all, they learned of the threat they believe Muslims pose from sources who were presented by the media as authoritative experts."

That rationale is absurd on at least three counts: first, it denies that individual Muslims are responsible for their own actions. Second, Ayaan Hirsi Ali is far more authoritative on the subject of female genital mutilation than anyone at the SPLC. Third, there's much more evidence linking the SPLC to hateful violence than there is for any link between Hirsi Ali—an award-winning human rights activist—and violence against anybody, much less Muslims (though radical Islamists have threatened *her*). In 2011, a fervent left-winger named Floyd Lee Corkins walked into the Family Research Council with a plan to shoot the conservative employees who worked there, and then—having murdered them—wipe Chick-fil-A sandwiches in their faces. A heroic security guard was all that prevented a massacre. After his arrest, Corkins told authorities that he chose the conservative nonprofit from the SPLC's list of "hate groups."[7] Yet, despite the fact that the SPLC's inaccurate characterization of a Christian group almost caused the mass murder of its employees, the SPLC still had the gall to accuse Ayaan Hirsi Ali of being a violence-inciting "extremist." And when the SPLC was called out for its falsehoods, the group refused to admit that it was wrong.

In April 2018, the SPLC finally removed the "anti-Muslim extremist" list that had been on its website for nearly two years. It did so because of threats of legal action from another individual on the list, Maajid Nawaz, himself a Muslim. The SPLC's Heidi Beirich gave a speech at Duke University where she claimed that Nawaz "believes that all mosques should be surveilled. In other words, his opinion is that all Muslims are potential terrorists." Both of those statements are false, and not only is Nawaz not an extremist, combating extremism has been a focal point of his career.[8] The SPLC's falsehoods were so blatant that the group agreed to settle Nawaz's suit for $3.3 million in damages, in addition to removing Nawaz's name from its website and publicly apologizing to him. The SPLC still hasn't offered a similar apology to Hirsi Ali.

The smear jobs against Hirsi Ali and Nawaz weren't isolated incidents. The SPLC routinely smears conservatives and other critics of left-wing identity politics because that's how the group makes money. Ultra-wealthy leftists write massive checks to the SPLC to demonstrate their wokeness because the SPLC is to identity politics what Planned Parenthood is to abortion. In August 2017, Apple CEO Tim Cook pledged $2 million to the SPLC, prompting Hirsi Ali to criticize Cook in a *New York Times* op-ed, saying that the SPLC was "an organization that has lost its way" and that now engages in "smearing people who are fighting for liberty."[9] Nevertheless, the SPLC's fear-mongering is a lucrative operation, and one that's tax-exempt to boot. The SPLC has more than $400 million in assets, including a cool $90 million stashed in offshore funds.[10] Liberal donors keep signing checks, and the SPLC keeps churning out smears as if it's their job—because it is.

In February 2018, the SPLC tried to smear respected liberal feminist scholar Christina Hoff Sommers as an extremist, because she's an open critic of left-wing identity politics. "In a report on 'Male Supremacy,' an ideology that the group says 'advocates for the subjugation of women,' it included American Enterprise Institute scholar Christina Hoff Sommers, calling her someone 'who gives mainstream and respectable face to some [Men's Rights Activist] concerns,'" the *Weekly Standard* reported.[11]

"This is a group I used to admire. They once went after Klan members and Nazis and now…[they go after] people like Ben Carson and Ayaan Hirsi Ali. It's absurd," Sommers told the *Standard*, adding: "They're blacklisting in place of engaging with arguments. They blacklist you, rather than try to refute you."[12] Dr. Ben Carson, who now serves as the Secretary of Housing and Urban Development under President Trump, was labeled an anti-gay "extremist" by the SPLC in October 2014 for stating his belief that marriage is a religious sacrament that occurs between a man and a woman.[13] To most people, Carson is not an extremist, but an inspiring real life example of the American Dream. He was raised in inner city Detroit by a single mother, and could easily have ended up in prison: at age fourteen, for instance, he tried to stab a classmate.[14] But he reformed himself, overcame the odds, and became an award-winning neurosurgeon, thanks to support from his mother, who pushed her sons to prioritize education and their Christian faith. In short, Ben Carson is an American success story that should inspire each and every one of us. But he, too, was labeled an extremist for simply stating the traditional Christian belief that marriage is the sacramental union of a man and a woman. The SPLC kept Carson's name on its list of "extremists" for four months before negative publicity finally convinced the SPLC to remove it.[15]

While the SPLC's smear artists have repeatedly lied about conservatives, they've also lied about themselves and what they represent. This became apparent in March 2019, when the SPLC fired its cofounder Morris Dees for unspecified "conduct issues." Two weeks later, SPLC president Richard Cohen resigned. Current and former SPLC employees accused the organization of turning a blind eye to corruption, sexual harassment, and racial discrimination within its own ranks.[16] In a scathing essay published in the *New Yorker*, former SPLC staffer Bob Moser described the SPLC as a "highly profitable scam" that was "ripping off donors."[17] Working at the SPLC, Moser wrote, came with "the guilt you couldn't help feeling about the legions of donors who believed that their money was being used, faithfully and well, to do the Lord's work in the heart of Dixie. We were part of the con, and we knew it."[18]

Despite all this, Google still uses the SPLC to help police hate speech on YouTube as part of YouTube's "Trusted Flagger" program. The SPLC and other third-party groups work closely with YouTube's employees to crack down on "extremist" content in two ways. First, the flaggers are equipped with digital tools allowing them to "mass flag" content for review by YouTube personnel. Second, the groups act as guides to YouTube's content monitors and engineers who design the algorithms policing the video platform. Google helps fund the SPLC as well, including $250,000 it gave the group in 2016 to promote "inclusion" and sponsor "a total redesign of the [SPLC's] Teaching Tolerance website to ensure teachers can more easily access and integrate the content into their lessons."[19] Among other things, the SPLC's "Teaching Tolerance" program promotes left-wing domestic terrorist Bill Ayers (formerly of the Weather Underground) as "a highly respected figure in the field of multicultural education."[20]

Just as the SPLC has a special relationship with Google, so too does it have a special relationship with Amazon. Amazon grants the

SPLC broad policing power over its Amazon Smile charitable program, which allows customers to identify a charity to receive 0.5 percent of the proceeds from their Amazon purchases. Customers have given more than $8 million to charities through the program since 2013, according to Amazon. Only one organization both participates in the Amazon Smile program and gets to determine who else is allowed to join: the SPLC. "We remove organizations that the SPLC deems as ineligible," an Amazon spokeswoman told me in May 2018.[21] Amazon grants the SPLC that power "because we don't want to be biased whatsoever," she said, though she couldn't comment on whether Amazon considers the SPLC to be fair and unbiased.

Of course, the reality is that the SPLC is entirely partisan and unfair. For example, Christian legal groups like the Alliance Defending Freedom (ADF) are barred from the Amazon Smile program, while openly antisemitic groups are included.[22] In January 2019, the Center for Immigration Studies (CIS), a non-partisan think tank supporting reduced immigration, sued the SPLC for labeling it a "hate group."[23] The lawsuit noted that the SPLC's "hate group" designation barred CIS from participating in the Amazon Smile program, which might very well have been part of the point.

Where Google and Amazon go, other Internet and social media sites follow. Even Spotify partnered with the SPLC to police "hate content."[24] And of course so does Facebook. The SPLC is on a list of "external experts and organizations" that Facebook works with "to inform our hate speech policies," Facebook spokeswoman Ruchika Budhraja told me in June 2018.[25] Publicly, the SPLC has lashed Facebook for not doing enough to police "hate speech" on the platform. "Harmful and hateful rhetoric on Facebook is not without consequence," a May 2018 SPLC report stated.[26] The report did not disclose the SPLC's working partnership with Facebook.

Twitter listed the SPLC as a "safety partner" that works with the tech company to combat "hateful conduct and harassment." The SPLC isn't the only left-wing group that bullied its way into influencing Twitter's speech policies, either. Twitter partners with dozens of other organizations as part of its "Trust and Safety" initiative. Almost all of them are left-wing. The Dangerous Speech Project, for example, is a member of Twitter's "Trust and Safety Council." The group's purpose, you'll be shocked to learn, is combating "dangerous speech." Feminist Frequency, a left-wing political group, is another one of Twitter's "online safety partners." Twitter's "hateful conduct and harassment" partners—a separate council from the "Trust and Safety Council"—includes the Dangerous Speech Project (again) and Hollaback! (a feminist group that supports greater online censorship).

To its credit, Twitter cut ties with the SPLC in March 2019, but Facebook, Amazon, and Google have not.

The Factually Challenged Fact-Checker

Snopes is a left-wing online publication with an awful track record on political fact-checking—which is exactly the opposite of what you want from a neutral political fact-checker. Snopes is okay at debunking tabloid stories about UFOs being spotted in Haiti[27] or scientists creating half-human, half-animal hybrids in the Amazon jungle,[28] but when it comes to serious news stories, Snopes struggles. Part of the problem is that Snopes hires from the fringes of the left-wing blogosphere, and its political fact-checks consistently resemble a defense of left-wing narratives.[29] For example, Snopes defended Democrats after they were criticized for the lack of onstage American flags on the first day of the Democratic National Convention in July 2016. Flags were on display for the Pledge of Allegiance and the national anthem, and then carried off-stage. On the convention's second day, in response to the criticism, the Democrats filled the stage with American flags. Those are the facts. They are undisputable. But Snopes acted as Democratic spin doctor. It rated the claim that "No American flags were on display at the 2016 Democratic National Convention" as "false," and as proof used an image from day two of the convention and attempted to pass it off as an image from day one.[30] That's not checking facts—it's inventing them.

Snopes performed a similar service for the Democrats in March 2017. During President Trump's first address to Congress, he paid tribute to Carrie Owens, the widow of Navy SEAL Ryan Owens who had been killed in action days before the speech. Owens received two separate standing ovations during the president's tribute to her husband's courage and her family's sacrifice. Two Democratic members of Congress, Keith Ellison of Minnesota and Debbie Wasserman Schultz of Florida, remained seated during the second standing ovation. Again, those are simply the facts. The video of the address is indisputable. But Snopes said claims that Ellison and Wasserman Schultz sat during the *second* standing ovation were "false" because they stood and clapped during the *first* standing ovation. After criticism, Snopes significantly revised its "fact-check," but didn't append an editor's note acknowledging its previous error.[31]

In February 2017, Snopes botched a fact-check of two former Planned Parenthood employees who stated—on the record—that Planned Parenthood offered bonuses to its employees if they hit certain abortion quotas. In an attempt to undermine one of the former employees' claims, Snopes said that she had recently lost a lawsuit against Planned Parenthood alleging widespread Medicaid fraud. That was wrong: the lawsuit was ongoing.[32]

Time and again, Snopes has demonstrated its untrustworthiness as a political fact-checker. But Snopes is still a fact-checker for Google, giving it priority placement in search results, and is an official fact-checking partner for Facebook. Google News includes Snopes in a special bar highlighting its approved fact-checking partners, and Facebook marks stories from Snopes with a "Fact-checker" badge.[33] When I reached out to Facebook in December 2016, a company spokeswoman stressed that the Snopes partnership was a pilot project.[34] More than two years later, Snopes is still an arbiter of truth for Facebook, even as Snopes' errors continue to pile up.

In March 2018, for example, Facebook threatened to suppress the Babylon Bee, a popular satirical website comparable to The Onion, after Snopes "fact-checked" one of its satirical articles titled "CNN Purchases Industrial-Sized Washing Machine To Spin News Before Publication." So eager was Snopes to protect CNN that it "fact-checked" this article and proclaimed it false, prompting Facebook to threaten Babylon Bee founder Adam Ford with demonetization and reduced viewership if the satirical website continued publishing "disputed info." Facebook later retracted the threat and apologized, but it continues to rely on the unreliable Snopes.[35]

In December 2018, a picture circulated on Twitter of Trump standing with members of his administration and congressional Republicans. Many of those pictured had a red X stamped over their faces, which Snopes stated meant they had lost their 2018 midterm reelection bids, because they had voted to repeal Obamacare. But not only had many of those marked with an X won reelection, some weren't even members of Congress.[36]

Snopes ludicrously claimed that its post was still "mostly true" because the number of Xs was roughly equivalent to the number of defeated Republicans who had voted to repeal Obamacare. *Politico* reporter Jake Sherman noted that Snopes' accuracy was "not really a question," because it "was nearly 100 percent wrong."[37] Nevertheless, Facebook marked Snopes' misleading article with the blue "fact-checker" badge and Google News highlighted it on its front page.

A month later, Snopes did it again. Nathan Phillips, the Native American activist who demonstrably lied about being harassed by a group of high school kids from Covington Catholic School at the 2019 March for Life, was discovered to have lied about something else, too: his military record. In interviews, Phillips described himself as a "Vietnam-times veteran" and in a 2018 Facebook video explicitly claimed that he was a Vietnam veteran who served "in theater." He told *Vogue* that "You know, I'm from Vietnam times. I'm what they call a recon ranger. That was my role."[38] Military records showed that Phillips never deployed to Vietnam, spent most of his military service as a refrigerator technician, and had gone absent without leave three times. He also had a criminal record that included assault.[39]

Phillips' lies were an embarrassment to the liberal media establishment that had fallen over itself praising him and condemning the Covington high school kids. But swooping in to the rescue was Snopes, which labeled the *fact* that Phillips had falsely claimed to be a Vietnam veteran as "unproven." And once again, Facebook's blue "Fact-Checker" badge accompanied Snopes' inaccurate "fact-check."

The pattern repeated itself in October 2019, when Snopes butchered its fact check of a left-wing smear of Chick-fil-A.[40] A left-wing Twitter user falsely blamed Chick-fil-A for proposed (and quickly scuttled) legislation in Uganda that would have provided the death penalty for homosexuality. "Today Uganda announced a bill to legalize murdering gay people. National Christian [Foundation] paid a preacher to go to Uganda and help their lawmakers with the bill. Chick-fil-a funds National Christian Org. If you eat at Chick-fil-a, this is what your money goes to," the tweet stated. That was false, but the tweet quickly went viral in left-wing Twitter circles anyway, garnering more than 57,000 retweets.[41] The NCF, for context, is one of the country's largest Christian nonprofits and provides funding to thousands of Christian charities and churches, including some that operate in Uganda. There's no evidence to support the claim that the NCF was orchestrating the proposed legislation, and was no evidence that Chick-fil-A was currently funding the NCF—but Snopes rated the false tweet a "mixture" of truth and fact in its "fact check." Egregiously, the Snopes article butchered basic facts, claiming that the Winshape Foundation, a charity founded by the chicken restaurant's owners, was funding the NCF. I checked the WinShape Foundation's publicly available tax documents, and they showed that show that NCF donated to WinShape Foundation in 2017 (the most recent year available), not the other way around.[42] Far from debunking misinformation, Snopes amplified it. Big Tech is doing nothing to advance media credibility—or its own credibility—by deputizing partisan "fact-checkers" like Snopes. It's the journalistic equivalent of hiring a raging alcoholic to watch your six pack of beer.

Media Matters

Media Matters is a far-left activist group that aims to muzzle prominent conservatives. One of Media Matters' specialties is whipping up advertiser boycotts against Fox News hosts like Sean Hannity, Tucker Carlson, and Laura Ingraham. It also led the successful effort to get conservative writer Kevin Williamson fired from *The Atlantic* just days after he was hired.[43]

Like the SPLC, Media Matters is focused entirely on attacking people on the right. And like the SPLC, it is hypocritical. For instance, Media Matters' president, Angelo Carusone, has his own trail of offensive online posts disparaging a number of minority groups.[44] In one post, Carusone wrote that his boyfriend was attractive "despite his jewry." In another, he ranted about an article on a "tranny" gang in Bangladesh:

Uhhh. Did you notice the word attractive? What the fuck is that doing in there? Is the write[r] a tranny lover too? Or, perhaps he's trying to justify how these trannies tricked this Bangladeshi in the first place? Look man, we don't need to know whether or not they were attractive. The fucking guy was Bangladeshi. And while we're out, what the hell was he doing with $7,300 worth of stuff. The guy's Banladeshi! [sic][45]

Do I think those blog posts should disqualify Carusone from a media career? No, I don't. The reality of human nature is that people are flawed and make mistakes. But by the Media Matters standard, Carusone should be permanently barred from public discussion for those posts. But he's not. Instead, Carusone uses his position to urge boycotts of right-of-center voices, using a standard that he himself couldn't pass.[46]

Carusone's organization targeted Fox News host Laura Ingraham for tweeting an article about David Hogg, the Parkland student-turned gun control activist, who had complained about not getting accepted into colleges like UCLA. Ingraham added "and whines about it," and said the result was predictable considering UCLA's acceptance rates. She later apologized to Hogg and invited him onto her show. (He rejected both the invitation and her apology.) Was her tweet insensitive? Sure. But if you were to make a list of offensive things cable news hosts have said over the years, Ingraham's tweet wouldn't crack the top 100. MSNBC host Mika Brzezinski later derided Secretary of State Mike Pompeo as a dictator's "buttboy" on national television, and nobody came for her advertisers. CNN commentator Bakari Sellers said Covington student Nick Sandmann deserved to be "punched in the face."[47] Sellers' CNN colleague, Symone Sanders, mocked Sandmann for his performance in an interview.[48] Neither Media Matters nor anybody else launched a boycott of CNN's advertisers. Even so, Hogg and Media Matters demanded that companies boycott Ingraham's show. Hogg's participation was excusable, considering that he was a senior in high school, but there's no excuse for the adults who pushed a teenager into doing their political dirty work for them.

Media Matters is expanding its dishonest boycott campaign beyond cable news. In a January 2017 memo circulated to donors. Media Matters outlined a strategy to prevent President Donald Trump's reelection in 2020 by enlisting Big Tech to help destroy conservative media. "Key right-wing targets will see their influence diminished as a result of our work," the memo assured donors. According to leaked documents, Media Matters intends to pressure Google (including YouTube) and Facebook to work with them to stifle conservative media.[49] In April 2018, Media Matters briefed left-wing donors and Democratic bigwigs on the changes it wants to enforce at Facebook, Google, and YouTube.[50]

One of its successes was getting a pledge from Facebook, after months of haranguing, to downrank "provocative" Facebook groups and pages. By Media Matters' standards, any conservative could be considered "provocative" if not "extremist." Media Matters published a list of alleged "extremist figures" attending the Trump White House's social media summit in July 2019. The list included the Heritage Foundation, a prominent conservative think tank.[51] To anybody familiar with Heritage, the "extremism" charge was laughable. Heritage is synonymous with the conservative establishment. In fact, Heritage *is* the conservative establishment. If they're "extremists," so is everybody to the right of Mitt Romney.

The Alex Jones Moment

And then there is Alex Jones. Jones, for those who don't know him, is the founder of the conspiracy website Infowars, and an all-around terrible person. He spread lies about the families of the children murdered at Sandy Hook Elementary School in 2012, accusing them of staging the whole thing. He knew full well that he was telling lies about suffering people, and he did it anyway. When Jones's ex-wife brought up his off-the-rails behavior in a custody battle, his legal defense was that he doesn't actually mean the crazy things he says, and that he adopts a public "persona," like a professional wrestler[52]—which makes the lies he tells about people even worse. In short: Alex Jones is a deeply immoral person. But he didn't burst onto the scene in 2016—he's been around for a long time. People who had moral objections to what he was saying for decades didn't try to silence him then. In the online free speech battle, Jones's grotesque behavior became a tool for leftists seeking to change how social media companies operate.

Within the span of a day in August 2018, YouTube, Facebook, and Apple all permanently banned Jones from their platforms. The first to move against Jones were YouTube and Facebook. Apple was the first major platform to ban him entirely, at which point most other tech companies followed suit.[53] Twitter showed relatively more restraint than its fellow tech giants, in that the company waited a month before it permanently banned Jones from the platform.[54]

I feel no sympathy for Alex Jones (other than for his soul) and he has no absolute right to use a company's platform. But what is troubling about the multi-platform purge of Alex Jones is the way he was banned—by left-wing activists and the liberal establishment media demanding that Big Tech act as a censor. The best way to hold Alex Jones accountable for libel is to take him to court, as the Sandy Hook families have done in a lawsuit that is ongoing. If, however, you want to use Alex Jones to change how social media operates, you highlight his outrageousness and the size of his audience as proof that tech companies need to change the rules. "It won't stop at Alex Jones," one Facebook insider told me. "It's unprincipled and not deriving from anywhere, so it's just subject to different concrete examples, where it's 'oh look this happened and oh this group is upset about this and they have a petition,' and eventually it leads to a place where you aren't allowed to say anything 'offensive' to anyone on the platform." And who determines what's offensive? Left-wing outrage mobs.

"Jones is undeniably an almost uniquely toxic figure. Slandering the Sandy Hook families by suggesting their dead children were nothing but 'crisis actors' was grotesque. And Jones has a long history of buffoonery, including but not limited to 9/11 trutherism. But I can't support banning him from ostensibly content-neutral platforms, and those who refuse to see this as the first step toward a more aggressive campaign of de-platforming conservatives are being obtuse," *Washington Free Beacon* editor Sonny Bunch wrote in an op-ed following Jones' purge. "The math here is simple: There is a growing belief that speech can be considered violence, that racist speech is by definition violence and that conservative thought is inherently racist. I don't need a whiteboard or lizard people to connect the dots."[55]

"So we're now trusting the capitalist class, massive, unaccountable corporations, to decide on our behalf what we may listen to and talk about? This is the take-home message, the terrible take-home message, of the expulsion of Alex Jones' Infowars network from Apple, Facebook, and Spotify and of the wild whoops of delight that this summary banning generated among so-called liberals: that people are now okay with allowing global capitalism to govern the public sphere and to decree what is sayable and what is unsayable. Corporate censorship, liberals' new favourite thing—how bizarre," British columnist Brendan O'Neill observed in *Spiked* magazine. "It doesn't matter what you think of Jones. It doesn't matter if you think he is mad, eccentric, and given to embracing crackpot theories about school shootings being faked. You should still be worried about what has happened to him because it confirms we have moved into a new era of outsourced censorship," O'Neill added. "It shows that what was once done by the state is now done by corporations. The illiberal, intolerant cleansing from public life of ideas judged to be offensive or dangerous has shifted from being the state's thing to being the business elite's thing."[56]

"Facebook today exercises government-like powers of censorship despite the fact that it is a private company. The *New York Times* or the *Wall Street Journal* can in effect censor Alex Jones by refusing to carry his content. But because there is a pluralistic and competitive market in traditional print media, this doesn't matter; Jones's followers can simply choose different media outlets. The same is not true in today's social media space," American political scientist Francis Fukuyama wrote afterwards. "I personally find Alex Jones completely toxic and am not unhappy to see his visibility reduced; that will be good for our democracy. But I am also very uncomfortable with a private quasi-monopoly like Facebook making this kind of decision."[57]

But those who expressed concern about Jones' ban were in the minority among the political and media class.

Almost as soon as the Jones precedent was set, liberal activists and Democratic politicians demanded it be applied more broadly. Democratic Senator Chris Murphy of Connecticut seized the opportunity to push Big Tech to go even further in their censorship. "Infowars is the tip of a giant iceberg of hate and lies that uses sites like Facebook and YouTube to tear our nation apart. These companies must do more than take down one website" Murphy wrote on Twitter. He insisted that the "survival of our democracy" depends on extreme censorship from Big Tech.[58]

Steven Crowder

To understand how the Jones formula will be applied, look at what happened to conservative comedian Steven Crowder. On May 30, 2019, Vox writer Carlos Maza, a former Media Matters staffer, posted a compilation of off-hand insults Crowder had directed at him across dozens of videos. "So, I have pretty thick skin when it comes to online harassment, but something has been really bothering me," Maza began. "Since I started working at Vox, Steven Crowder has been making video after video 'debunking' Strikethrough [Maza's video series]. Every single video has included repeated, overt attacks on my sexual orientation and ethnicity." If Maza wanted to complain about Crowder calling him "lispy queer" and "gay Latino from Vox," he would have been well within his rights to do so. The best way to counter speech you don't like is more speech—not censorship. But Maza wasn't looking to rebut Crowder—he was looking to silence him. Maza and like-minded journalists launched a full-blown advocacy campaign, demanding YouTube ban Crowder from the platform. YouTube originally ruled that Crowder's videos didn't violate its policies. After six days of lobbying from the media and liberal YouTube employees,[59] YouTube demonetized Crowder's channel.

They're Coming for Ben Shapiro

If there's one certainty in the digital speech battles, it's this: the mob is going to come for Ben Shapiro. Ben is by far the most effective voice on the right. He bridges the gap between think-tank conservatism and populist conservatism better than anybody. Congressmen read his work and listen to his podcast—but so do the people outside the political world. I know D.C. insiders who listen to Ben's podcast every day—and I know EMTs in Texas who do too. Ben reaches everybody—from the beltway to the border. That's why the activist left is going to do everything they can to deplatform him. They're already laying the groundwork with bad faith smear efforts.

The *Washington Post* published an op-ed by Media Matters researcher Talia Lavin, who attacked Shapiro and others in a piece titled, "How the Far Right Spread Politically Convenient Lies about the Notre Dame Fire." (Lavin, it's worth noting, joined Media Matters after losing her fact-checking job at the *New Yorker* magazine for falsely accusing an Immigration and Customs Enforcement officer of being a Nazi.[60]) In her *Post* op-ed, Lavin couldn't actually point to any lies Shapiro told, but she claimed that some of his tweets mentioning Judeo-Christian values "evoked the specter of a war between Islam and the West that is already part of numerous far-right narratives." Actually, Shapiro didn't mention Islam at all in the tweets, but why let facts get in the way of a good narrative? After all, this isn't about honestly assessing the facts—it's about silencing the right's most effective voices.

In August 2019, Media Matters published a video compilation intended to portray Shapiro's Daily Wire website as extremist. But Ben, knowing how Media Matters and other such outlets operate, was one step ahead of the smear artists. In July 2018, he posted an article on the Daily Wire titled, "So, Here's A Giant List Of All The Dumb Stuff I've Ever Done (Don't Worry, I'll Keep Updating It)."[61] In it, he listed everything—every comment, every article, every tweet—liberal hatchet men could try to use against him. He broke it down into four categories: "Stupid/Immoral Stuff I've Said (And Usually Retracted Multiple Times)," "Stuff The Left Is Taking Out Of Context," "Stuff The Left Doesn't Like That Happens To Be True," and "Controversial Opinions That The Left Just Doesn't Like." It was a brilliant move, but it's not going to be enough to keep left-wing activists from trying to—if not succeeding in—censoring him and the Daily Wire. Media Matters pays people to watch

Ben's daily podcast and selectively edit clips of his show to make him look bad.

Change the Terms

Six left-wing groups, spearheaded by the SPLC and the Center for American Progress (which is funded by liberal mega-donors like George Soros[62]), formed a pro-censorship coalition in October 2018. The coalition, "Change the Terms," is trying to pressure all service-hosting tech companies into establishing rules against "hate speech"—not just on Facebook, Google, and Twitter, but on crowdfunding sites and website-hosting companies like GoDaddy. "Internet companies must do more to ensure that they are doing their part to combat extremism and hate, and take the threat of hate and extremism on their platforms more seriously," the SPLC's Heidi Beirich said in the announcement about the new censorship coalition. The SPLC pledged to hound social media platforms into compliance.

"To ensure that companies are doing their part to help combat hateful conduct on their platforms, the SPLC and other organizations in this campaign will track the progress of major tech companies—especially social media platforms—to adopt and implement these model corporate policies. Then, in the following year, the organizations will provide report cards to those companies on both their policies and their execution of the policies," the SPLC's announcement promised. The coalition demanded that all tech companies follow Google's lead in establishing "trusted flaggers" to flag questionable individuals, organizations, and statements. More than that, they want tech companies to deny their platforms to people who engage in unacceptable *off-platform* behavior.[63]

In other words, the SPLC and a variety of other left-wing groups want privileged access to Big Tech's levers of power in order to police the off-platform behavior of their opponents. The terms also require tech companies to "establish a team of experts on hateful activities with requisite authority who will train and support programmers and assessors working to enforce anti-hateful activities, elements of the terms of service, develop training materials and programs, as well as create a means of tracking the effectiveness of any actions taken to respond to hateful activities." The demand is essentially for tech companies to adopt the "anti-bias" teams now popular on college campuses. "Create a committee of outside advisers with expertise in identifying and tracking hateful activities who will have responsibility for producing an annual report on effectiveness of the steps taken by the company." Big Tech already answers to the left-wing hacks at the SPLC, but the hacks want it guaranteed in writing.

And give them this: it's working. In late 2018 the fundraising site Patreon (used by Jordan Peterson and others) agreed to implement the recommendations of "Change the Terms." Leftists then leapt into action identifying people that, according to them, were in violation of the new rules. It's a shrewd play that they intend to replicate across platforms until the Internet resembles a giant MSNBC panel—with leftists and liberals facing off against a few milquetoast conservatives (the sort approved of by the *New York Times* and the *Washington Post*) who will be expected to agree with them.

It's about Power

The fact that massive companies like Google and Facebook work with dishonest partisan hacks like Snopes and the SPLC shows how little they truly care about problems like misinformation and political extremism. It's not about those things—it's about power. That's why progressives melt down anytime conservatives get close to any kind of influence within Big Tech: they know just how much damage you can inflict on your political enemies when working those crucial levers of power. That's why left-wingers at Facebook have worked so furiously to try to push Joel Kaplan out of his job as a Facebook vice president, and why they're intent on making sure Facebook only partners with third-party organizations that toe the left-wing line.

In 2018, Facebook was slowly revamping its content policies, and in an effort to get conservative critics off its back, it hired Refiners, the public relations arm of the GOP opposition research firm America Rising. Refiners pointed out to conservative media that several groups criticizing Facebook were funded by left-wing billionaire George Soros.[64] That was true, but it was also inconsequential: were conservatives really supposed to stop criticizing Facebook for its anti-conservative bias just because Soros-funded activists were also criticizing Facebook? In reality, what Facebook had accomplished was sidelining the premier Republican opposition research firm from being one of its critics. Meanwhile, the Soros-backed Media Matters complained that Facebook wasn't being left-wing enough and launched a petition that demanded that the *Weekly Standard* be dropped as a fact-checker for the platform, because the high-brow (and establishment Republican, anti-Trump) magazine was allegedly a "right-wing publication with a history of partisan lies."[65] The petition asserted that "Facebook has no place partnering with the outlet to provide neutral and independent analysis." To Media Matters, left-wing outlets like Snopes are nonpartisan, but center-right outlets like the *Weekly Standard* are "right-wing" and untrustworthy, despite being independent enough to be enormously critical of Trump.

Media Matters no doubt felt vindicated when the *Weekly Standard* fact-checked and dinged the Soros-backed left-wing blog ThinkProgress. During the confirmation hearings for Supreme Court Justice Brett Kavanaugh, ThinkProgress published an article titled "Brett Kavanaugh Said He Would Kill Roe v. Wade Last Week and Almost

No One Noticed." The headline is pretty much what the article argued, but it didn't actually include any evidence of Kavanaugh saying he would overturn the Supreme Court ruling. The *Standard*'s fact-check labeled the claim "false," and ThinkProgress writers proceeded to have a meltdown, as did most of the liberal media establishment.

But William Saletan, writing at Slate.com, made a crucial observation:

> So the *Standard's* fact check is correct. By itself, that's a small point. But ThinkProgress and its allies have made the dispute into something much bigger. By attacking the fact check as biased on the grounds that a conservative magazine published it, they've proved the opposite of what they intended. They've confirmed that the press is full of left-leaning journalists who sometimes can't see or acknowledge congenial falsehoods, and they've demonstrated how these journalists unite, when challenged, in a tribal chorus to accuse conservatives of trying to "censor" them. In sum, they've demonstrated why we need conservative journalists to help check facts.[66]

That is obviously true, but within much of Big Tech and certainly within the liberal media establishment it is also controversial because neither one really cares about neutral reporting or an honest assessment of the facts. They care much more about advancing an ideological narrative. It is about politics; it is about power; and the left does not want its media dominance challenged.

CHAPTER EIGHT

The Narrative

The establishment liberal media has a huge incentive to control or be the biggest player on social media. The digital revolution has made some of the traditional media's functions irrelevant. People don't need to buy a newspaper or watch the evening news to find out what tomorrow's weather will be. They can check the weather on their phones within three seconds. People no longer need to buy classified ads in a newspaper. They can do the same on Craigslist for free or next to nothing. Social media companies present a direct threat to establishment media companies by eating up consumers' attention (attention that could be directed towards MSNBC or CNN) and the ad revenue that comes with it. And even then, establishment media companies are at a disadvantage.

Because tech companies constantly vacuum up your data, advertisers can target highly specific demographics on social media platforms. That advantage is crucial. Buying time on MSNBC allows companies to advertise to people who watch Rachel Maddow. But buying ads on Twitter or Facebook allows them to target the specific subset of Rachel Maddow fans who are most likely to buy their products. Newspapers, cable networks, and digital media companies simply can't compete with that ad model. The best they can do is try to succeed within it—or play dirty.

The digital advertising market falls into two categories: 1) Google and Facebook 2) everybody else. Google and Facebook together account for nearly 60 percent of the digital advertising market.[1] Massive amounts of money are at stake: by 2023, the digital advertising industry is projected to be worth $230 billion—that's billion, with a "b."[2] And establishment media companies feel entitled to Big Tech's ad revenue. Not only that, they also demand that Big Tech prevent conservative media outlets from profiting off their platform. The size of the digital advertising market is crucial context in considering corporate media companies' coverage of Google and Facebook. Media coverage of widespread misinformation or "hate speech" on tech platforms inflicts damage on Google and Facebook's ad revenue. The solution always involves Big Tech giving Big Media a greater market share.

In June 2019, the *New York Times*, for example, hammered Google News with a story that bordered on propaganda. The story was headlined: "Google Made $4.7 Billion from the News Industry in 2018, Study Says," and made the case that Google was a leech on traditional news media.[3] The story was, however, egregiously misleading. Columbia Journalism Review writer Mathew Ingram noted, "As it turns out, the report was published by the News Media Alliance, a media-industry lobby group formerly known as the Newspaper Association of America, and the figure quoted by the *Times*—without any critical assessment whatsoever—appears to be based almost entirely on questionable mathematical extrapolation from a comment made by a former Google executive more than a decade ago."[4]

The News Media Alliance, the special interest group behind the junk study, was at the same time lobbying in favor of a law exempting print and online media companies from antitrust regulations. Among the special interest group's members: the *New York Times*. The paper's garbage article "was timed in such a way as to provide maximum publicity for a bill that the New Media Alliance has been promoting to Congress, called the Journalism Competition and Preservation Act," Ingram observed. The bill "would allow print and online news companies to cartelize into a united front against Google and Facebook....Under the new law, which would sunset in four years, the cartel could collectively withhold content from Google, Facebook and other sites and negotiate the terms under which the two tech giants could use their work. Anti-trust law currently prohibits such industrywide collusion," noted *Politico*'s Jack Shafer.[5] In other words, the *Times* made a lobbying pitch, disguised as a news article, based on shoddy data from a special interest group whose members include the *Times*, for a bill that would benefit the paper's interests. It was a gross move—but illuminating in demonstrating how establishment media's business interests are intertwined with their coverage of Big Tech.

Social media provided journalists with the ability to reach millions of people they couldn't reach before, but it gave everyone else that ability too—a democratizing effect that was good for alternative media outlets, but bad for corporate media behemoths used to having an institutional advantage. It was also bad for out-of-touch establishment reporters who feel entitled to Americans' trust, whether they've earned it or not. Social media poses a direct threat to traditional media companies, and many journalists openly resent Facebook and Google because of it.

They resent not only the loss of advertising revenue, but the loss of power. The 2016 election showed that establishment media journalists no longer controlled the national discussion the way they felt they should. The national media was so uniformly "With Her" that they viewed Clinton's loss as proof positive that voters must have been misled by other news sources. Social media is the biggest reason why establishment media outlets don't have the smothering level of influence they once enjoyed, and it took the 2016 election for them to realize it.

When establishment media companies stoke fears about social media platforms being sources of misinformation, they do so out of self-interest. In the 1930s, newspapers had the same incentives to discredit radio. The most celebrated case was probably the famous Orson Welles radio broadcast of *The War of the Worlds*, which included a fictional newsman warning about an alien invasion. Legend has it that across the country, people listening to the broadcast panicked en masse. But that was newspaper spin; it's not what actually happened.

"The supposed panic was so tiny as to be practically immeasurable on the night of the broadcast. Despite repeated assertions to the contrary in the PBS and NPR programs, almost nobody was fooled by Welles' broadcast," Jefferson Pooley and Michael J. Socolow wrote in a 2013 *Slate* article.[6]

"How did the story of panicked listeners begin? Blame America's newspapers. Radio had siphoned off advertising revenue from print during the Depression, badly damaging the newspaper industry. So the papers seized the opportunity presented by Welles' program to discredit radio as a source of news. The newspaper industry sensationalized the panic to prove to advertisers, and regulators, that radio management was irresponsible and not to be trusted."

Now consider the establishment media's alarmist treatment of tiny fake news websites.

Fake News about Fake News

Two days after the 2016 election, *The Guardian* published a news article titled, "Facebook's Failure: Did Fake News and Polarized

Politics Get Trump Elected?" The sub-headline: "The company is being accused of abdicating its responsibility to clamp down on fake news stories and counter the echo chamber that defined this election." Subtle. The fear-mongering article was shared more than 26,000 times.[7] "The most obvious way in which Facebook enabled a Trump victory has been its inability (or refusal) to address the problem of hoax or fake news," claimed Max Read of *New York Magazine*.[8] A month after Trump's victory, MSNBC's Brian Williams confidently informed his viewers that "fake news played a role in the election." Actual research on the subject, rather than partisan hysteria, shows it was highly, highly, *highly* unlikely that "fake news" influenced the election.[9] The people who share fake news aren't swing voters: they're the most diehard supporters of all. They're the people who *want* to believe fake news. But if you only get your news from establishment news sources, you probably have a much different picture of fake news' (non-existent) influence.

Both the *New York Times* and the *Washington Post* cited fake news site DenverGuardian.com in December 2016 as a frightening example of the dangers of an unpoliced Facebook. At the time, DenverGuardian.com wasn't in the top 91,000 sites ranked by web traffic in the United States, according to web analytics firm Alexa. To put that number in perspective: the site that supposedly helped elect President Trump was more than 84,000 slots behind the website for Northern Virginia Community College. The *New York Times* devoted front-page coverage to another fake news site called the "Patriot News Agency." The *Times'* story gravely emphasized that "operators of Patriot News had an explicitly partisan motivation: getting Mr. Trump elected." But the Patriot News Agency was even less popular than DenverGuardian.com, clocking in all the way down at 184,898 in Alexa's ranking of websites in the United States. And the site's Facebook page had barely 100 likes at the time, giving it roughly the same reach on Facebook as your local coffee shop.[10] Of course those facts didn't make it into media coverage.

In a study published two years later, professors from Princeton and the University of Michigan provided further confirmation that "fake news" was essentially a non-issue in the 2016 and 2018 elections.[11] University of Michigan professor Brendan Nyhan, the lead political scientist on the study, noted in February 2019: "it turns out that many of the initial conclusions that observers reached about the scope of fake news consumption, and its effects on our politics, were exaggerated or incorrect. Relatively few people consumed this form of content directly during the 2016 campaign, and even fewer did so before the 2018 election." Nyhan added: "there remains no evidence that fake news changed the result of the 2016 election." Nyhan said the media would be better off focusing on "elite misinformation," rather than "fake news." But for the establishment media, the real issue was taking back control of the national discussion.

When CNN hosts and commentators in the liberal establishment media talk about the 2016 election and "misinformation," it's obvious which voters they believe were "misinformed." They don't mean Hillary Clinton voters—they mean the voters who think differently than they do. The near universal equivalence in the establishment media between "misinformation" and right-wing voters ignores the fact that there's plenty of evidence of widespread misinformation on the left. For example, polling has consistently shown that a majority of Democratic voters believe that Russia altered voting totals to give Trump a fraudulent victory, which, given all the evidence and government statements to the contrary, is Alex Jones level fake news.[12] And yet, you never hear that fact brought up on CNN, or covered by the *Washington Post* or the *New York Times*.

In April 2018, *Business Insider* published a story, picked up by many establishment media outlets, including the *Washington Post*, claiming that Russian "bots" (automated accounts) were rallying around Fox News host Laura Ingraham.[13] Bret Schafer, communications director for the bipartisan Alliance for Securing Democracy, told me in April 2018 that most of the reporting on the story was "inherently inaccurate." And he should know, because the *Business Insider* story cited the Alliance's own Hamilton 68 Dashboard, which tracks online misinformation. "Most notably, and this is the most common error, we don't track bots, or, more specifically, bots are only a small portion of the network that we monitor," Schafer said. "We've tried to make this point clear in all our published reporting, yet most of the third party reporting on the dashboard continues to appear with some variation of the headline 'Russian bots are pushing X,'" he said. In fact, the alleged flood of Russian bot-generated tweets in support of Ingraham oftentimes amounted to no more than a couple dozen tweets.[14]

But Russian bot stories are candy for left-wing audiences and useful to establishment media narratives. CNN sent a cameraman and a reporter to the front lawn of an elderly female Trump supporter whose group had been promoted by Russian Internet trolls.[15] She had no idea that a Russian group had been involved, but after CNN's coverage, she received a flood of threats and vicious messages.[16] Curiously, the network didn't give the same treatment to left-wing filmmaker Michael Moore, who was duped into attending an anti-Trump protest organized by Russians after Trump's election.[17] In fact, not only did CNN not ambush Moore at his house, they didn't cover the story at all. Neither did CNN cover the fact that an arm of the Women's March was also duped into promoting Russian propaganda.[18]

The establishment media has a narrative—for instance, that Trump voters are misinformed, that Russian bots are rescuing pro-Trump Fox News hosts, and that Trump supporters are inherently racist—and sticks to it. That's one of the reasons why the national media screwed up the Covington Catholic story so catastrophically. They were predisposed to assume that conservative high school students wearing Make America Great Again caps, had to be the bad guys, when in fact *they* were the victims of harassment. It's also why left-wing extremists—including violent, far-left Antifa—receive minimal or even sympathetic coverage. On both TV and social media, CNN's Chris Cuomo claimed that Antifa's critics were too hard on the group; and in one tweet, Cuomo actually compared Antifa thugs to American soldiers on D-Day (both, he argued, were fighting fascism).[19] When a group of Antifa thugs jumped two Marines in Philadelphia in December 2018, however, Cuomo did not comment on the story. The attackers reportedly hurled racial slurs at the Marines, both of whom are Mexican-Americans, while beating them bloody. In Cuomo's (sort of) defense, he wasn't alone: CNN's entire network ignored the Antifa attack. It didn't fit the establishment media's narrative about extremists existing solely on the right.

Facebook took down hundreds of accounts in August after cybersecurity investigators identified Iranian operatives running a covert influence campaign, similar to the one waged by Russian trolls in 2016. Among the investigators' findings: Iranians trolls were trying to promote Vermont Sen. Bernie Sanders.[20] CNN covered the fact that Facebook took down the Iranian accounts, but its coverage left out the Iranians' support for Bernie, who has been a vocal supporter of the Obama administration's much-criticized Iran deal. The story provided a stunning contrast with CNN's hysterical coverage of Russian trolls.

Establishment media silence on left-wing misinformation campaigns is the rule—not the exception. In 2018, when North Dakota Democrats ran a misinformation campaign meant to keep hunters from voting,[21] CNN didn't cover it at all. When left-wing billionaire Reid Hoffman funded a misinformation campaign to boost

Democrats in the 2017 Alabama special election and the 2018 midterm elections, CNN was uninterested. In the special election, Reid-funded activists staged a self-described "false flag" operation to link Republican Senate candidate Roy Moore to "Russian bots" and created misleading Facebook pages linking Moore to alcohol prohibitionists. Former Obama administration official Mikey Dickerson played a key role in organizing the misinformation operation, which was titled "Project Birmingham." That all sounds pretty newsworthy, but CNN didn't devote a second of airtime to the story or publish a single story on its website about it.[22] When it emerged that Reid-funded operatives garnered millions of impressions on Facebook during the 2018 midterm elections, CNN again ignored the story because the establishment liberal media narrative insists that misinformation is only a problem on the right. The more the establishment media, and left-wing media, can make "misinformation" and conservatism synonymous, the more they can demand the exclusion of conservative news organizations from Facebook. In July 2018, at a meeting between Facebook and several national media companies, Buzzfeed editor Ben Smith decried the fact that half of the outlets represented leaned to the right. HuffPost editor in chief Lydia Polgreen echoed Smith, and both singled out the Daily Caller as an outlet that Facebook should have excluded from the meeting. The meeting was supposed to be off the record, but details leaked to the *Wall Street Journal*, which published a story headlined, "Publishing Executives Argue Facebook Is Overly Deferential to Conservatives."[23] Smith's temper tantrum came less than three months after Zuckerberg had assured him that Facebook would slowly "dial up" the suppression of some outlets while boosting others.[24] Facebook's sin was not giving liberal outlets preferential treatment fast enough.

BuzzFeed and the HuffPost are openly partisan. The HuffPost, for instance, published a news article—not an opinion column, a news article—that called on Democrats to pack the Supreme Court once they retook political power.[25] "It is time for the Democratic Party to stop pretending that the words of men like [former Supreme Court Justice Anthony] Kennedy matter as much as their actions. The Supreme Court, Congress, and the executive branch of the U.S. government are instruments of political power. All three are currently being used to advance the ideology and agenda of international fascism," wrote HuffPost senior reporter Zach Carter, presumably with a straight face.[26] Buzzfeed, meanwhile, canceled ads from the Republican National Committee, and used data collected on its own users to help create ads to support Democrats.[27] A 2016 analysis by the left-leaning media watchdog Fairness and Accuracy In Reporting (FAIR) found BuzzFeed's coverage of Obama was "almost uniformly uncritical and often sycophantic" to the extent that it was "99 percent uncritical—and borderline creepy."[28]

Concurrent with trying to dismiss conservative news outlets as sources of "misinformation," the establishment liberalmedia has gone into overdrive in promoting itself as the fact-based, neutral arbiter of truth. "Like firefighters who run into a fire, journalists run towards a story," MSNBC host Katy Tur said in a network promotion that was widely mocked. CNN has built a marketing campaign around the slogan, "Facts First." The *Washington Post* adopted the slogan "democracy dies in darkness." The *New York Times* created its own tagline for the Trump era: "Truth. It's more important now than ever." (The obvious implication: truth isn't so important when liberals win elections.)

But in fact, the establishment media has dramatically lowered the bar for accuracy, and a staggering number of "bombshells" in the Trump era have turned out to be duds. In January 2017, the *Washington Post* broke a sensationalist story, informing readers that the Russians had hacked into the United States power grid through a company in Vermont. Except they hadn't. A piece of malware was found on a single laptop at the company, which wasn't connected to the power grid. The *Post*'s reporters didn't reach out to the power companies before publishing their fear-mongering report. It was just one of those stories that was just too good to check; and besides it allegedly involved Russian hackers.[29] In May 2017, CNN reported that Attorney General Jeff Sessions had wrongly failed to disclose meetings with Russians in his capacity as a senator. Six months later, CNN walked back that report: actually, Sessions hadn't done anything improper after all.[30]

In June 2017, CNN led the media pack with a salacious scoop that former FBI director James Comey in his testimony to Congress would refute Trump's claim that Comey had told him three separate times that he wasn't under investigation. But CNN's exclusive report was inaccurate—instead, Comey confirmed Trump's claim.[31] Later that month, CNN published another explosive scoop: Trump adviser Anthony Scaramucci was under investigation for his ties to Russian influence operations. The problem with the story, of course, was that Scaramucci was under no such investigation, or any investigation at all. Three CNN reporters lost their jobs over that botched story.[32] In September 2017, NBC News reported that former Trump campaign chair Paul Manafort's notes included the word "donation" near the words "Republican National Committee,"[33] stoking speculation that Russians had funneled money to support Trump's campaign—except that the story was bunk, based on anonymous and apparently misinformed sources.[34]

In December 2017, Brian Ross at ABC News had his own bombshell-that-wasn't when he reported that former Trump adviser Michael Flynn was prepared to testify that Trump ordered him to make contact with the Russians before the 2016 election. Ross's report shocked the political world and sent stock markets plunging, but there was a flaw in the story—it wasn't true.[35] This misfire bomb-shell was so egregious that ABC had to suspend Ross for four weeks.

That same month, Bloomberg dropped its own bombshell: Spe-cial Counsel Robert Mueller had "zeroed in" on Trump and had subpoenaed bank records for Trump and members of his family.[36] That story, too, was incorrect. Bloomberg later walked back its report, saying instead that somebody in Trump's circle had had their bank records subpoenaed, which is not exactly a shocking revelation within the context of an FBI investigation. Not to be outdone, CNN flubbed its own December 2017 bombshell. The network reported that Donald Trump Jr. had seen emails stolen by Russian hackers ten days before WikiLeaks released them—only, it turned out, he hadn't.[37] In January 2019, BuzzFeed reported that Robert Mueller had documents in his possession showing that Trump had directed his former personal lawyer, Michael Cohen, to lie to Congress about Trump's desire to build a hotel in Moscow during the 2016 cam-paign.[38] Talking heads on CNN and MSNBC discussed whether Trump would be impeached based on the BuzzFeed report.[39] But BuzzFeed got it wrong. Robert Mueller's office, known among reporters for its consistent silence on stories about the investigation, took the nearly unprecedented step of issuing a public statement slapping down the BuzzFeed report.

The hoopla surrounding Michael Wolff's book on the Trump White House, *Fire and Fury*, provides yet another case study of media hypocrisy. Prominent members of the establishment media readily accepted Wolff's book when it came out in January 2018, even though Wolff himself undermined the accuracy of his sourcing by conceding in a note at the start of the book that parts of it had a general "looseness with the truth, if not with reality itself."[40] That admission was arguably the most truthful part of Wolff's book, which was filled with errors and untruths. One gossipy anecdote claimed that Senate majority leader Mitch McConnell blew off a meeting with President Trump to get a haircut. Dozens of political journalists had heard that rumor well before Wolff's book came out, including me. I personally ran down that same tip months before and found it didn't hold up. But Wolff decided to run with it and wrote the rest of his book the same way.

Portions of *Fire and Fury* were distributed early to *The Guardian*, which published breathless articles on Wolff's claims. What happened next, in the words of CNBC's Marty Steinberg (who showed more skepticism than most), was a "journalistic feeding frenzy."[41] CNN's Brooke Baldwin gushed about the "bombshell details" and "the myriad shockers" in the book.[42] Her network devoted repeated segments to questioning the president's fitness for office, based on reports in Wolff's book.[43] A minority of journalists noted Wolff's errors. Matt Drudge, as always, was ahead of the crowd, calling Wolff's work "fabricated bullshit."[44] *New York Times* White House correspondent Maggie Haberman more or less agreed: "The details are often wrong. And I can—I can see several places in the book that are wrong."[45] But most of the establishment media ran with the fake-but-accurate narrative. MSNBC's Joe Scarborough told his million-plus viewers[46] that, regardless of the factual accuracy, the book "rings true."[47] His MSNBC colleague, Katy Tur, noted that despite the criticisms, Wolff's book "did feel true." She pointed to "a lot" of the book that "reads true, that feels true."[48] "There's disappointment about the errors that are in the text, but the book itself does hold up," added CNN's Brian Stelter, who hosts a show called "Reliable Sources."[49] Wolff's book was tabloid-level sensationalism, full of half-truths and outright falsehoods; it was, in short, misinformation, yet prominent members of the establishment media helped propel *Fire and Fury* to the top of the *New York Times* best-seller list, where it remained for weeks.

It showed, if there was any doubt, that the liberal establishment media is intent on controlling the national narrative. And the establishment media wants its narrative to control social media as well.

CHAPTER NINE

What Comes Next

In Europe and in authoritarian states like China and Venezuela, tech companies are already using their awesome power to stifle the flow of information, in some cases to silence political dissent and to keep pro-censorship authorities happy.

■   ■   ■

Cologne, Germany: During New Year's celebrations, in the first few hours of 2016 in Germany, as many as 1,200 German women and girls were sexually assaulted. The perpetrators were largely young, male migrants from Arab and North African countries.[1] That's not a political statement—it's a fact.

The rampant sexual assault and harassment was a predictable result of German Chancellor Angela Merkel's open-door immigration policy to Syrian and Iraqi refugees, Brookings Institute fellow James Kirchick argued in his 2017 book *The End of Europe.* "No woman who has ever walked the streets of a major Arab city—nor any man who has ever accompanied one—could have expressed shock at this turn of events. Blatant street harassment is simply the norm in much of the Arab world," observed Kirchick, a respected foreign correspondent and no extremist on immigration matters. Kirchick pointed out that a "2013 study conducted by the United Nations Entity for Gender Equality and the Empowerment of Women found that 99.3 percent of women in Egypt—the most populous Arab country—have experienced sexual harassment, half of them on a daily basis. So prevalent is mass, participatory sexual assault in this part of the world that there is a word for it, *taharrush*, one with which Europeans have become painfully acquainted as this distinctly Arabian pathology has been imported to their streets."[2]

Mass sexual assaults of German women and girls by thousands of migrants who had recently immigrated to Germany without being vetted was politically disastrous to Merkel and her party, who had staked their credibility on their controversial open-doors policy. The attacks undeniably would not have occurred if Merkel hadn't broken with longstanding immigration policy and authorized mass entry. So, rather than openly discussing the incident, Cologne authorities tried to keep the public in the dark about the politically inconvenient mass rape and sexual assault of their wives, sisters, and daughters. But those facts slowly trickled out, drip by drip, and the number of victims ticked ever higher. It took more than six months for the public to learn the full story. A police report obtained by German newspaper *Süddeutscher Zeitung* in July 2016 finally revealed the full, horrifying scale of the mass attacks.

Fast forward two years to New Year's Eve 2018 in Germany. When the clock struck midnight, it rang in both the new year and a new German censorship law that requires social media companies to delete "illegal hate speech" immediately—within 24 hours of posting—or risk a 50 million euro fine.[3] The Cologne police department, earnestly trying to avoid a repeat of the mass attacks against women in the city, tweeted out safety bulletins in Arabic. That didn't sit well with Beatrix von Storch, a right-wing member of German Parliament.[4] Ms. von Storch slammed the police on social media and accused them of pandering to "barbaric, gang-raping Muslim hordes of men." Her message was inflammatory, but it didn't come out of nowhere—von Storch was addressing a real issue that had irreparably affected the lives of thousands of Germans. Roving rape gangs assaulted six hundred women in Cologne alone in a single night.[5] And the problem was not contained to a single night, either: a study released in January 2018 found that young, male refugees in Germany are driving a violent crime spike across the country.[6]

But just because an issue is real, that doesn't mean Facebook will allow you to have a real conversation about it. Tech companies quickly deleted von Storch's posts, as well as posts that quoted von Storch's posts. Even comedians who posted satirical tweets about von Storch's censored posts were themselves censored.[7]

Von Storch wasn't the only female member of Parliament to trip over the new speech rules. Alice Weidel, another right-wing politician, was similarly disgusted by what she viewed as a concession by the Cologne police. She wrote on Twitter: "Our authorities submit to imported, marauding, groping, beating, knife-stabbing migrant mobs." Twitter deleted Weidel's post as well. Apparently, in this instance, the progressive position on hate speech was to err on the side of censoring women who were outraged about mass gang rapes. And profit-driven tech companies, seeking to avoid massive fines, agreed.

For those who care about free speech, it was easy to see the censorship coming. Reporters Without Borders, a press freedom organization, expressed alarm about the German bill when it was proposed. "The short deadline for removal, coupled with the threat of heavy fines, will very likely drive social networks to remove more content than is legally justified. Even journalistic publications will face a real danger of being affected by this kind [of] over-blocking without due process," said the organization's executive director in Germany, Christian Mihr. Mihr implored German politicians to shelve the legislation, saying, "This hastily-drafted bill should be adjourned and only decided upon after national elections this coming fall and after thorough consultations with civil society. This applies especially true for the crucial question under which conditions content will have to be removed."[8] His warnings were ignored.

There's no indication that German authorities plan to change anything, even as tech companies engage in overly broad censorship as a result of the new law. As it stands, it's a massive blow to free speech in Germany, a country which some ostensibly smart pundits have claimed is now the leader of the free world.[9]

■   ■   ■

The rest of Europe is following Germany's lead in attempting to control their citizens' online speech. As Google's "good censor" memo approvingly noted: "governments are taking steps to make online spaces safer, more regulated, and more similar to their offline laws. Protected from hate speech on the street? Now you are on the net too...."

In the United Kingdom police officers now act as online speech cops to combat "hate speech"—a term so expansive that it includes posting rap lyrics and not complying with transgender pronoun mandates.

What's that look like? Scottish YouTuber Markus Meechan was convicted in March 2018 of a hate crime for training his girlfriend's pug to do Nazi salutes and to react to antisemitic phrases like "gas the Jews" in a video he posted to YouTube. Meechan, known online as Count Dankula, said his goal was to turn his girlfriend's small dog into the "least cute thing I could think of"—an antisemitic pug.[10] After a lengthy court process, Meechan was fined the rough equivalent of $1,100.[11] "As a matter of law, the test is not whether the video was offensive but whether it was grossly offensive. That standard is an objective one in which I must apply the standards of an open and just multi-racial society, taking account of context and the relevant circumstances, applying reasonably enlightened contemporary standards, considering whether the message is liable to cause gross offence to those to whom it relates: in this case, Jewish people. It is a high test. I concluded, applying these standards to the evidence, that your video was not just offensive but grossly so, as well as menacing, and that you knew that or at least recognised that risk," Sheriff Derek O'Connell wrote in his sentencing order.[12] "The fact that you claim in the video, and elsewhere, that the video was intended only to annoy your girlfriend and as a joke and that you did not intend to be racist is of little assistance to you. A joke can be grossly offensive," O'Connell wrote.

Nineteen-year-old Liverpool woman Chelsea Russell was convicted of a hate crime over an Instagram post.[13] Her crime: including offensive rap lyrics in an Instagram tribute to a friend who had recently passed away. An anonymous tipster sent a screenshot of one of Russell's Instagram posts to authorities, at which point Russell "was brought in for questioning," the Crown Prosecution Service (CPS) wrote in an announcement.[14] Russell denied the post was offensive but "Police Constable Dominique Walker, who works in the Hate Crime Unit, gave evidence that the terms Ms. Russell had used were 'grossly offensive' to her as a black woman and to the general community." The CPS authorized police to charge Russell with "sending by a public communication a grossly offensive message.... The district judge agreed with us and found her guilty. The CPS applied for the sentence to be uplifted as it was a hate crime. The district judge agreed with this too and increased the sentence from a fine to a community order," CPS announced. Russell was sentenced to eight weeks of community service, ordered to pay roughly $900 in penalties, and given an eight-week curfew.[15]

Meechan and Russell are far from alone in facing government inquisitions over social media posts. British Home Secretary Amber Rudd in October 2017 announced "a new national hub to tackle the emerging threat of online hate crime." The official announcement promised that the hub would be operational within months and would "help drive up the number of prosecutions."[16] As it was, British authorities arrested nine people a day in 2016 for "posting allegedly offensive messages online as police step up their campaign to combat social media hate speech," British newspaper *The Times* reported that same month.[17] That made for a 50 percent rise in arrests in just two years, the paper noted.[18] In September 2018, the South Yorkshire police urged residents to report offensive online comments made by their fellow citizens, whether or not they constituted a hate crime. "In addition to reporting hate crime, please report non-crime hate incidents, which can include things like offensive or insulting comments, online, in person or in writing," the police department wrote on Twitter.[19] Police in Hertfordshire, England, arrested Kate Scottow, a thirty-eight-year-old mother, in front of her children in December 2018 because she referred to transgender activist Stephanie Hayden as a man.[20] Hayden, a male who self-identifies as a transgender woman,[21] reported Scottow to authorities. Scottow was released with a warning for verbal harassment, after being detained for seven hours.[22] "We take all reports of malicious communication seriously," the police assured the public.[23]

In January 2019, police in Britain interrogated a man because he "liked" a humorous poem that authorities considered "transphobic."[24] The man, Harry Miller, told the BBC that a police officer told him that "even though I had committed no crime he needed to check my thinking." Reflect on that for a minute: the police needed to *check his thinking*. Orwell's Big Brother would be proud: thoughtcrime is on its way to becoming a real crime in the U.K.

In February 2019, a seventy-four-year-old Suffolk woman, Margaret Nelson, received a visit from police officers, who were concerned about some of her tweets and blog posts. The tweets that drew the attention of law enforcement included "Gender is BS. Pass it on," the U.K. *Spectator* noted.[25] "Gender's fashionable nonsense. Sex is real. I've no reason to feel ashamed of stating the truth," Ms. Nelson wrote in another tweet. "The bloody annoying ones are those who use words like 'cis' or 'terf' and other BS, and relegate biological women to a 'subset'. Sorry you believe the mythology.'" In one of the offending blog posts, titled "Death doesn't misgender. You die as you were born," Nelson wrote: "If a transgender person's body was dissected, either for medical education or a post-mortem examination, his or her sex would also be obvious to a student or pathologist. Not the sex that he or she chose to present as, but his or her natal sex; the sex that he or she was born with. Even when a body has been buried for a very long time, so that there is no soft tissue left, only bone, it is still possible to identify the sex. DNA and characteristics such as the shape of the pelvis will be clear proof of the sex of the corpse."[26] Nelson recounted the officer's visit: "The officer said she wanted to talk to me about some of the things I'd written on Twitter and my blog. She said that some of the things that I'd written could have upset or offended transgender people. So could I please stop writing things like that and perhaps I could remove those posts and tweets?" Nelson informed the officer she would do no such thing.

In September 2018, British Member of Parliament Lucy Powell of the Labour Party introduced legislation that would regulate even *private* Facebook groups and hold the groups' administrators responsible for what their members say. The law was necessary, Powell claimed without an ounce of self-awareness, because police couldn't monitor private conversations as well as they could monitor public tweets. "Because these closed forums can be given a 'secret' setting, they can be hidden away from everyone but their members. This locks out the police, intelligence services and charities that could otherwise engage with the groups and correct disinformation," she wrote in an op-ed touting her legislation in *The Guardian*.[27] "I believe we can force those who run these echo chambers to stamp out the evil that is currently so prominent."

Two months after Powell's announcement, Zuckerberg announced that Facebook would begin suppressing "provocative groups" and "provocative content" across all countries.[28] Tech companies have shown time and time again that they're willing to censor on behalf of governments or leftist groups if that's what it takes to protect profit margins.

The media and political establishments support crackdowns on online speech in Europe and in the United States, because social media represents a serious threat to them and to progressive priorities. Nigel Farage made this point to Mark Zuckerberg in a May 2018 letter blasting Facebook's algorithm changes. Without "Facebook and other forms of social media, there is no way that Brexit or Trump or the Italian elections could ever possibly have happened. It was social media that allowed people to get behind the back of mainstream media," Farage wrote.[29] "Now perhaps you're horrified by this creation of yours and what it's led to. I don't know," he continued. "But what is absolutely true is since January of this year, you changed your modus operandi, you changed your algorithms, and it has led directly to a very substantial drop in views and engagements for those who have got right-of-center political opinions."

In March 2018, French Prime Minister Edouard Philippe announced that France would pass its own version of Germany's online "hate speech" law and require social media platforms to delete "hate speech" within twenty-four hours or face severe fines.[30] The French government took matters even further eight months later. President Emmanuel Macron announced in November 2018 that his administration would "embed" regulators inside of Facebook to help combat "hate speech" on the platform.[31] One French official called the partnership between the government and Facebook an "unprecedented experiment."[32]

The European Parliament has even threatened to pass online hate speech legislation that is similar to the German bill and would impose online "hate speech" regulations and censorship across the entire continent.[33] The EU hasn't had to follow through on that threat, because Facebook, Google, YouTube, and Twitter quickly ramped up their censorship operations, much to the EU's delight.[34]

■　　■　　■

The rise of populist movements around the world and Big Tech's all-encompassing censorship regime are on a collision course. The European establishment's populist nightmare is just beginning: the underlying destabilizers of their liberal governments—societal trends like stagnating wages, changing demographics, and an increasing gap between ultra-wealthy elites and everyone else—aren't going away. These external pressures are only growing, and, at the same time, European governments are increasingly pressuring major tech companies to change their algorithms to combat populist forces. As populism spreads in Europe and as tech companies become cozier with European governments, the political establishment will pressure Big Tech to head off populist revolts like the "yellow vest" protests in France. Indeed, some of Big Tech's current censorship activities, like suppressing "provocative" groups and "polarizing" content, are designed to do just that. But reliance on these heavy-handed tactics produces a conundrum: the more tech companies intervene on behalf of the establishment, the more they risk feeding those same populist forces they're trying to thwart.

European leftists using Big Tech to silence political dissent are playing a dangerous game and establishing dangerous precedents, but for now they intend to exploit their influence over and within Big Tech as much as possible.

Big Tech Won't Save You

Communist China is a totalitarian regime that controls information and expression and tracks every aspect of its citizens lives. A vast network of security cameras outfitted with facial recognition technology, allows the state to identify virtually anyone walking the streets within minutes.[35] The government carefully tracks and meticulously documents everything from internet usage to credit card purchases, and feeds all this data into an algorithm that determines a "citizen score." Those with high citizenship marks are eligible to travel abroad and receive other benefits; low scores can result in even further restrictions on an individual's freedom.

But the Communist regime doesn't do it all on its own. The Chinese government uses social media companies as an arm of the surveillance state and pressures them to silence political dissidents. In

August 2017, for example, Chinese authorities cracked down on three of the most widely used social media companies in the country: WeChat, Weibo, and Baidu Tieba.[36] The Cyberspace Administration of China (CAC) said that the tech companies had allowed forbidden content, including "obscenity" and "false rumors," to proliferate on their platforms.[37] All three companies responded to this public reprimand by immediately hiring additional "content moderators" to increase censorship on their platforms.[38] As one story noted, while the app WeChat "is an all-encompassing system that does indeed make everyday life easier, it's also a powerful tool of government surveillance and control," that has even led to the arrest of users.[39]

Chinese authorities targeted the China-based news application Toutiao in a similar manner, because it allegedly wasn't doing enough to police content on its platform and was "causing a negative impact on public opinion online."[40] *Abacus*, the tech arm of the *South China Morning Post*, reported:

> For years, Toutiao maintained that it was just a platform, and said it wouldn't edit any content on the site—but that may be changing. State media criticised Toutiao for its reliance on algorithms to control what it shows users. And in December of 2017, authorities shut down Toutiao for 24 hours, accusing it of spreading "pornographic and vulgar content." Several days later, the company started recruiting 2000 content reviewers—saying "Communist Party members would be considered first."

Toutiao should have called it a "trusted flaggers" program. In addition to bringing in new speech monitors, the tech company also banned or suspended 1,100 bloggers accused of spreading "low-quality content."[41]

■   ■   ■

America's tech giants have signaled their willingness to cooperate with the Chinese Communist government when it comes to censorship. Google had secretly planned to build a Chinese search engine that met the regime's standards and would blacklist certain phrases like "human rights."[42] It only scuttled the agreement after details leaked to the public (though they haven't ruled out bringing it back).[43] In hindsight, when Google removed its signature motto "Don't be evil" from its code of conduct in April 2018, observers should have seen the writing on the wall.[44]

Facebook has not yet sold its corporate soul to the extent that Google has—but it's only a matter of time before it does. Facebook has already done underhanded things like trying to trick children into spending their parents' money. A January 2019 report from the Center for Investigative Reporting revealed that "Facebook orchestrated a multi-year effort that duped children and their parents out of money, in some cases hundreds or even thousands of dollars, and then often refused to give the money back."[45] Facebook also "encouraged game developers to let children spend money without their parents' permission—something the social media giant called 'friendly fraud'—in an effort to maximize revenues, according to a document detailing the company's game strategy," the report added. Perhaps the worst part of the incident, however, is that when Facebook employees discovered that some children were unwittingly spending their parents' money and created a fix for the problem, company executives shut it down.[46] Facebook is all about profit margins, and that's why it's open to doing business in China.

In an October 26, 2018, letter to the Senate Intelligence Committee, Facebook declined to rule out doing business with China, despite the Communist regime's totalitarian policies. Instead, Facebook promised that "rigorous human rights due diligence and careful consideration of free expression and privacy implications would constitute important components of any decision on entering China." The key phrase in the letter was that "no decisions have been made around the conditions under which any possible future service might be offered in China." In other words, Facebook was keeping its options open. Google and Facebook's willingness to do business with China's totalitarian regime makes a mockery of anyone who thinks that those companies will protect free speech in America. Google and Facebook won't protect you from pro-censorship politicians; they'll work with pro-censorship politicians to make sure they can keep profiting from your patronage. They're doing exactly that in Europe. And in the United States they have all too willingly caved to left-wing activists and their own left-wing employees who demand censorship.

America

The United States is different, of course, because our Constitution guarantees freedom of speech. While the First Amendment is undoubtedly threatened by "hate speech" laws and other progressive legislation, for now the major threat to free speech in the United States comes not from government-imposed censorship, but from left-wing activists, the liberal media that promotes them, and the corporate advertisers that fear them.

That censorship is already happening, and it doesn't just restrict what you see on social media. Virtually every medium for communicating information is subject to left-wing censorship. Spotify, for instance, recently banned PragerU from purchasing advertisements on its channels. The ban came six months after the music-streaming service announced that it was partnering with the SPLC to keep "hateful content" off its platform, a ban that apparently did not extend to popular rappers on Spotify. Microsoft provides yet another example. The Seattle-based software giant built a news tracker into the latest edition of its browser, Microsoft Edge.[47] The tracker, operated by start-up company NewsGuard, rates online news sources and their trustworthiness. Trustworthy sources get a green badge, untrustworthy news outlets' stories a get a red badge. NewsGuard's rating of right-wing news sites is split—the Daily Mail and Breitbart didn't make the "trustworthy" list, while the Daily Caller and *National Review* did—but the organization cleared almost every left-wing news source. HuffPost and Salon both received green ratings, as did Raw Story. ThinkProgress and Media Matters, which exist solely to push left-wing propaganda, also received green ratings.[48] Microsoft's left-leaning news monitor is an example of the future of digital news. It or something like it will inevitably be adapted by Google and Mozilla with fact-check apps and context bars to advance "smart browsing" and marginalize conservative voices.

In October 2018, the SPLC and Center for American Progress spearheaded a coalition of left-wing organizations demanding that *all* tech companies establish an advisory group of "trusted flaggers" to flag controversial individuals, organizations, and statements and promise to punish individual users for both on-platform and off-platform behavior that failed to meet their standards of acceptable speech. In other words, the left wants to decide who can use tech platforms and who can't. By making anything that breaks with progressive orthodoxy a de facto "controversy," progressives are seeking to create a digital environment where conservatives keep their views to themselves. That's taking censorship to a new level, but it's not unprecedented.

Adrian Chen, writing in the *New Yorker*, noted that conservatives have long felt excluded from the mainstream media. In the 1950s and 1960s when conservatives tried to establish their own radio stations, "their main obstacle was the F.C.C.'s Fairness Doctrine, which sought to protect public discourse by requiring controversial opinions to be balanced by opposing viewpoints. Since attacks on the mid-century liberal consensus were inherently controversial, conservatives found themselves constantly in regulators' sights."

He continued, "the Fairness Doctrine really was used by liberal groups to silence conservatives, typically by flooding stations with complaints and requests for airtime to respond. This created a chilling effect, with stations often choosing to avoid controversial material." Today, he adds, "The technical fixes implemented by Google and Facebook in the rush to fight fake news seem equally open to abuse, dependent, as they are, on user-generated reports."[49]

The strategy of the left-wing groups is obvious. They label conservative ideas as "hate speech," demand that Bisg Tech get on the right side of history and ban "hate speech," and make it a litmus test for advertisers ("is *your* company supporting hate speech?"). Sympathetic journalists describe these requests as reasonable instead of the naked political power grabs they are. And once a tech company caves to the pressure, it essentially deputizes the SPLC and other leftist groups to decide who can stay on its platform. And left-leaning employees at the tech companies will gladly be the internal enforcers of censorship. Just as college campuses have been overwhelmingly turned into giant "safe spaces" for leftists, free of disconcerting ideas or challenging arguments, the vast majority of tech platforms will likewise transform into digital safe spaces for progressive orthodoxy.

Democratic politicians have eagerly joined the left-wing campaign for censorship. The Democrat-dominated California state legislature passed a bill in August 2018 ordering the state attorney general to establish an advisory committee to combat "fake news" on social media. The bill, SB 1424, tasked the committee with two objectives: "a) Study the problem of the spread of false information through

Internet-based social media platforms; and b) Draft a model strategic plan for Internet-based social media platforms to use to mitigate the spread of false information through their platforms." One California legislator even proposed an amendment to SB 1424 that would have instructed the government-sponsored committee to draft "potential legislation for mitigating the spread of false information through social media, if the advisory group deems it appropriate."[50]

The bill was so extreme that even liberal watchdogs expressed alarm. "Government recommendations about how to discriminate among Internet speakers are harmful in and of themselves," the left-leaning Electronic Frontier Foundation warned.[51]

Governor Jerry Brown—a Democrat and a liberal, but more moderate than the leftists in the legislature—vetoed the bill on the grounds that he didn't think the committee was necessary. But Brown is now out of office, and the Democrats obtained a veto-proof legislative supermajority in the 2018 midterms, so bills reining in free speech online will likely make their way back through California's legislature.[52] Federal courts are all that stand in the way of bills like SB 1424 going into effect, and if Democrats eventually "pack the court," as progressive activists have demanded, the courts might not be enough. SB 1424 is not unique. One Democratic state assemblyman in California proposed legislation in 2017 to require public schools to teach students how to differentiate "fake news" from "real news."[53] That is, the state, perhaps advised by the likes of Media Matters and the SPLC, would instruct students on acceptable and legitimate news sources.

At the federal level, Democrats have already shown that they're willing to use government power to pressure Facebook into taking the steps they want. Democrats have used their majority in the House of Representatives to drag tech companies into committee hearings about "hate speech" and "misinformation" on their platforms. Even without passing any legislation, House Democrats can make life painful for tech companies who stand up for free speech online. As Matt Taibbi observed in *Rolling Stone*, "politicians are more interested in *using* than curtailing the power of these companies. The platforms, for their part, will cave rather than be regulated."[54]

Of course, the Democrats are willing to pass legislation, too, and liberal columnists are already laying the groundwork for Democrats to regulate Facebook, on the grounds that the company isn't doing enough to police speech on its platform.[55] One op-ed in the *Washington Post* argued that because Facebook had allegedly dropped the ball on "hate speech" too many times, Democrats had little other choice but to step in and solve the problem.[56]

■   ■   ■

"What concerns me is that major technology platforms today have the power to redefine the four corners of acceptable debate in the country," Florida congressman Matt Gaetz told me in a January 2019 phone interview. Gaetz has been one of the more vocal Republicans to express concern about online censorship trends. "I think that the marketplace of ideas should accommodate a wide range of views, including offensive views. And you know, I'm a libertarian by nature. I don't want Washington running my life, but I especially don't want Silicon Valley running my life," said Gaetz. "And, if you look at our politics today, we're a fifty-fifty country, Donald Trump is the president because he won three rust belt states by a point each. And so, if Silicon Valley can alter the debate even slightly, if they can, you know, they don't have to be able to mute conservative voices, they just have to be able to turn down the volume a hair, and it could have a substantial impact on the future of the world," he added.

Christians are especially vulnerable to censorship from big tech, said Gaetz. "I think the people that could be most at risk are people of faith. I think there is a movement within this country to label doctrinal elements of the Christian faith as hate speech. You would literally see a de-platforming of Christianity in the digital age if there is not greater transparency as to how content is treated online."

Left-wing activists aren't just coming for free speech—they're coming for religious freedom as well, and using Big Tech to do it.

CHAPTER TEN

What to Do

In the last decade, and particularly since the 2016 election, the digital landscape in America has lurched away from free speech and towards censorship, with left-wing partisans exercising an outsized role over who gets censored. Tech companies are transitioning from open platforms into tiered platforms, with different privileges for different speakers, with left-wing opinions and the liberal media establishment artificially elevated, and conservative opinions and alternative media outlets artificially minimized.

"There's always going to be one rule for the establishment and one rule for everybody else on social media now," tech reporter Allum Bokhari told me. "We see this with stuff like hate speech and harassment as well. Look at all the harassment and actual threats of violence we saw directed at the Covington kids on Twitter—nobody got banned, a few people had to delete tweets, nobody lost their blue checkmark, and then a few weeks later we saw mass bans against people telling journalists to learn how to code."[1] He added: "There's been this general power grab by elites who recognize that the Internet is a fundamental threat to their power because it decentralizes communications and gives everyone a massive platform and they want to do something about it."

Despite censorship and pressure from the establishment media, Bokhari thinks that decentralization will continue "because there's no really turning back the clock to a pre-digital era." Today, he says, "anybody can get a social media account and reach an audience of millions and progressives are right to be afraid of it because it totally takes away the power of the mainstream media organizations." That explains, he concluded, the "fear-mongering about fake news" and the demands that tech giants give preferential treatment to left-wing media. "I think we're going to see that continue up through 2020."

By undercutting and suppressing dominant right-of-center information sources—as tech companies have done—Big Tech is trying to put its thumb on the scales of public opinion. The question is: how much further—and how fast—will Big Tech go to manipulate the national discourse? Conservatives and other proponents of free speech are running out of time, but they do have ways to push back.

Make It Hurt

At their core, Facebook, Google, and Twitter are about one thing: making money. Tech giants silence conservatives not just because they want to, but because the left has made it financially painful for them not to crackdown on "hate speech" and "fake news." If conservatives want equal treatment from Facebook, Google, and Twitter they'll need to adopt the left's tactics and make the censorship of conservative voices costly to Big Tech. Conservatives are at a disadvantage because of the establishment media's and Big Tech's left-wing bias, but if conservatives are going to have any success in the future digital era, they will need to win this battle. That begins with making it embarrassing for Big Tech to censor conservative media. My email is at the end of this chapter—shoot me a tip anytime about cases of unfair digital censorship. I'm happy to help you make some noise.

And conservatives need to make noise. As Allum Bokhari said, decentralization in communication really can't be stopped—and conservatives need to take advantage of that. In this battle every conservative needs to be a citizen activist, and a citizen journalist. We need to defend first principles, like the First Amendment to the Constitution, and not let the left dismantle them with stalking horses about "hate speech." Conservatives need to stay—or get—involved on social media and support conservative news sites so that our voices will continue to be heard.

What conservatives should *not* do is abandon Big Tech platforms. That is simply surrendering—and conservatives do that far too often, which is why institution after institution, most egregiously in our colleges and universities, falls to the left. Nor should conservatives look to government for a solution. Certainly there are some benefits to *threatening* government action in order to win concessions from Big Tech. But it would be short-sighted for conservatives to support any law granting the government more influence over content-policing on social media, because what we need is less regulation of political speech, not more.

What made social media attractive to conservatives in the first place was that it offered a way to get around the liberal cultural establishment, which otherwise dominates the national conversation. During the healthcare debate, Senate Minority Leader Chuck Schumer fed television talk show host Jimmy Kimmel Democratic talking points, which Kimmel then parroted to his audience. Celebrities relish the chance to turn award shows into left-wing political rallies. Even sports commentators push gun control on-air.[2] The right doesn't have that range of cultural influence. What they had on social media was a single level playing field, where they could share their ideas. That's changing—and changing quickly—but conservatives still have a significant voice there.

Facebook, Google, and Twitter are profit-driven companies that care deeply about their public image. Their executives bend over backwards to appease liberal activists and journalists in part because they agree with them, and in part because they fear them. Until they fear conservatives just as much—and fear that the censoring of conservative viewpoints will cost them money—they will continue to do the work of the left—work that is directed at the end of free speech. Those are the stakes, and why conservatives must win.

Reach Peter J. Hasson at PeterJHasson@protonmail.com

Acknowledgments

Without the unconditional encouragement and support of my parents, Seamus and Mary Hasson, this book—indeed, my entire writing career—never would have been possible.

My six siblings and two siblings-in-law have also shaped me into the person and writer I am today, and I'll always be grateful for each one of them. I especially owe thanks to my older brother James, who read the earliest versions of this book and whose advice was crucial in making it sharper and more focused.

My fiancée Mairin is my rock and a constant source of joy in my life—and that was especially true throughout the often-grueling process of writing a book. I can't thank her enough for her love and support—and for the literal gallon of buffalo chicken dip she made for me while I was holed up in my apartment finishing the manuscript.

My best friend Tommy let me bounce ideas off him and reviewed my work throughout this entire process. He's the man.

The wonderful folks at Regnery Publishing believed in this project from the start over two years ago and helped make it better every step of the way.

I also owe thanks to Scott Niklason, Patrick Ryland, Dr. James Krueger, and Andrew Zwerneman, my high school Humane Letters teachers, for my early formation, and Rudy Bush, my journalism professor at the University of Dallas, who taught me the nuts and bolts of investigative reporting.

Last, but most important, thanks be to God, through whom all things are possible, and without whom, nothing is.

Notes

Chapter One: The Establishment vs. Free Speech

1. Matt Drudge, "Speech to the National Press Club on Media and the Internet," American Rhetoric Online Speech Bank, June 2, 1998, https://www.americanrhetoric.com/speeches/mattdrugdenationalpressclub.htm.
2. "2016 Richard S. Salant Lecture on Freedom of the Press," Audio & Video, Harvard Kennedy School, https://shorensteincenter.org/jeffrey-rosen-future-of-free-speech-in-a-digital-world/.
3. Catherine Rampell, "Liberal Intolerance Is on the Rise on America's College Campuses," *Washington Post*, February 11, 2016, https://www.washingtonpost.com/opinions/liberal-but-not-tolerant-on-the-nations-college-campuses/2016/02/11/0f79e8e8-d101-11e5-88cd-753e80cd29ad_story.html?noredirect=on&utm_term=.cc80c8bfa429.
4. Christopher Ingraham, "The Dramatic Shift among College Professors That's Hurting Students' Education," *Washington Post*, January 11, 2016, https://www.washingtonpost.com/news/wonk/wp/2016/01/11/the-dramatic-shift-among-college-professors-thats-hurting-students-education/?noredirect=on&utm_term=.93a840dd674a.
5. Bradford Richardson, "Democratic Professors Outnumber Republicans 10 to 1, Study Shows," *Washington Times*, April 26, 2018, https://www.washingtontimes.com/news/2018/apr/26/democratic-professors-outnumber-republicans-10-to-/.
6. Lance Izumi, "Why Are Teachers Mostly Liberal?" Pacific Research Institute, April 3, 2019, https://www.pacificresearch.org/why-are-teachers-mostly-liberal/.
7. Hadas Gold, "Survey: 7 Percent of Reporters Identify as Republican," *Politico*, May 6, 2014, https://www.politico.com/blogs/media/2014/05/survey-7-percent-of-reporters-identify-as-republican-188053.
8. Eric Wemple, "Dear Mainstream Media, Why So Liberal?" *Washington Post*, January 27, 2017, https://www.washingtonpost.com/blogs/erik-wemple/wp/2017/01/27/dear-mainstream-media-why-so-liberal/?noredirect=on&utm_term=.6fa6aa24ba23.

9. Kirsten Powers, *The Silencing: How the Left Is Killing Free Speech* (Washington. DC: Regnery, 2015), 70.

10. Andrew Sullivan, "Is Intersectionality a Religion?" *New York Magazine*, March 10, 2017, http://nymag.com/intelligencer/2017/03/is-intersectionality-a-religion.html.

11. Jennifer Brett, "New York Mayor Bill de Blasio Calls for Chick-fil-A Boycott," Atlanta Buzz Blog, https://www.ajc.com/blog/buzz/new-york-mayor-bill-blasio-calls-for-chick-fil-boycott/KbXzNqHpJUoKsCWgNRgkTK/.

12. Ashley Feinberg, "Leak: *The Atlantic* Had a Meeting about Kevin Williamson. It Was a Liberal Self-Reckoning," HuffPost, May 3, 2018, https://www.huffingtonpost.com/entry/leak-the-atlantic-had-a-meeting-about-kevin-williamson-it-was-a-liberal-self-reckoning_us_5ac7a3abe4b0337ad1e7b4df.

13. Rachel Lu, "Why Conservatives Don't Become Professors," *National Review,* June 2, 2016, https://www.nationalreview.com/2016/06/conservative-professors-academia-liberal-nicholas-kristof/.

14. Stanley Kurtz, "Year of the Shutdown: It Was Worse Than You Think," *National Review,* May 31, 2017, https://www.nationalreview.com/corner/year-shout-down-worse-you-think-campus-free-speech/.

15. Peter Beinart, "A Violent Attack on Free Speech at Middlebury," *The Atlantic,* March 6, 2017, https://www.theatlantic.com/politics/archive/2017/03/middlebury-free-speech-violence/518667/.

16. Peter Hasson, "Seattle City Council Candidate Drops Out of Race, Citing Harassment of His Wife," Daily Caller, November 14, 2018, https://dailycaller.com/2018/11/14/seattle-council-chris-rufo-wife-harassment/.

17. James Antle, "Violence against Trump Supporters: Who Is to Blame," *National Interest,* June 3, 2016, https://nationalinterest.org/feature/violence-against-trump-supporters-who-blame-16464.

18. PragerU, "War on Boys," YouTube, May 19, 2014, https://www.youtube.com/watch?v=OFpYj0E-yb4.

19. Lesley Stahl, "Facebook 'Embeds,' Russia and the Trump Campaign's Secret Weapon," CBS News, June 10, 2018, https://www.cbsnews.com/news/facebook-embeds-russia-and-the-trump-campaigns-secret-weapon-60-minutes/.

20. Reid Wilson, "Final Newspaper Endorsement Count: Clinton 57, Trump 2," *The Hill,* November 6, 2016, https://thehill.com/blogs/ballot-box/presidential-races/304606-final-newspaper-endorsement-count-clinton-57-trump-2.

Chapter Two: Rigged

1. Aaron Smith, Monica Anderson, "Use of Different Online Platforms by Demographic Groups," Internet and Technology, Pew Research Center, March 1, 2018, http://www.pewinternet.org/2018/03/01/social-media-use-2018-appendix-a-detailed-table/.

2. Elisa Shearer, Jeffrey Gottfried, "News Use Across Social Media Platforms 2017," Journalism and Media, Pew Research Center, September 7, 2017, http://www.journalism.org/2017/09/07/news-use-across-social-media-platforms-2017/.

3. John Shinal, "Mark Zuckerberg: Facebook Can Play a Role That Churches and Little League Once Filled," CNBC, June 26, 2017, https://www.cnbc.com/2017/06/26/mark-zuckerberg-compares-facebook-to-church-little-league.html.

4. Smith, Anderson, "Use of Different Online Platforms."

5. Laura Sydell, "On Its 7th Birthday, Is Twitter Still the 'Free Speech Party,'" All Tech Considered, NPR.org, March 21, 2013, https://www.npr.org/sections/alltechconsidered/2013/03/21/174858681/on-its-7th-birthday-is-twitter-still-the-free-speech-party.

6. Josh Halliday, "Twitter's Tony Wang: 'We Are the Free Speech Wing of the Free Speech Party,'" *The Guardian,* March 22, 2012, https://www.theguardian.com/media/2012/mar/22/twitter-tony-wang-free-speech.

7. Noam Cohen, "The Truth about Facebook's Fake Quest To Connect the World," Wired.com, December 3, 2018, https://www.wired.com/story/facebook-mark-zuckerberg-fake-quest-to-connect-the-world/.

8. Allum Bokhari, "The Good Censor-GOOGLE LEAK," Scribd.com, https://www.scribd.com/document/390521673/The-Good-Censor-GOOGLE-LEAK.

9. Bokhari, "The Good Censor"

10. Alyssa Newcomb, "Twitter CEO Jack Dorsey on Alex Jones, Election Security and Regrets," NBC News, August 15, 2018, https://www.nbcnews.com/tech/tech-news/twitter-ceo-jack-dorsey-alex-jones-election-security-regrets-n900931.

11. "Transcript of Mark Zuckerberg's Senate Hearing," The Switch, *Washington Post,* April 10, 2018, https://www.washingtonpost.com/news/the-switch/wp/2018/04/10/transcript-of-mark-zuckerbergs-senate-hearing/?noredirect=on&utm_term=.a584ff40a471.

12. Farai Chideya, "Nearly All of Silicon Valley's Political Dollars Are Going to Hillary Clinton," FiveThirtyEight, October 25, 2016, https://fivethirtyeight.com/features/nearly-all-of-silicon-valleys-political-dollars-are-going-to-hillary-clinton/.

13. Rachel Stoltzfoos, "19 Insane Tidbits from James Damore's Lawsuit about Google Office Environment," The Federalist, January 10, 2018, https://thefederalist.com/2018/01/10/19-insane-tidbits-james-damores-lawsuit-googles-office-environment/.

14. "New Lincoln Network Survey Shows Conservatives Feel Uncomfortable in Silicon Valley Workplaces," Bold, February 2, 2018, https://bold.global/bold-staff/2018/02/02/new-lincoln-network-survey-shows-conservatives-feel-uncomfortable-silicon-valley-workplaces/.

15. Mike Wacker, "Former Google Engineer: How Google Discriminates against Conservatives," Daily Caller, August 19, 2019, https://dailycaller.com/2019/08/19/wacker-google-discriminates/.

16. Peter Hasson, "Exclusive: Facebook, Amazon, Google and Twitter, All Work with Left-Wing SPLC," Daily Caller, June 6, 2018, http://dailycaller.com/2018/06/06/splc-partner-google-facebook-amazon/.

17. "SPLC Statement on Dr. Ben Carson," Southern Poverty Law Center, February 11, 2015, https://www.splcenter.org/sites/default/files/d6_legacy_files/downloads/publication/splc_statement_carson_feb2015.pdf.

18. Rich Lowry, "The SPLC Designates Itself," *National Review,* March 19, 2019, https://www.nationalreview.com/2019/03/southern-poverty-law-center-weaponized-political-correctness/.

19. Marc Thiessen, "The Southern Poverty Law Center Has Lost All Credibility," *Washington Post,* June 21, 2018, https://www.washingtonpost.com/opinions/the-southern-poverty-law-center-has-lost-all-credibility/2018/06/21/22ab7d60-756d-11e8-9780-b1dd6a09b549_story.html.

20. Peter Hasson, "Exclusive: YouTube Secretly Using SPLC To Police Videos," Daily Caller, February 27, 2018, http://dailycaller.com/2018/02/27/google-youtube-southern-poverty-law-center-censorship/.

21. Peter Hasson, "SPLC Confirms They're Helping Police Videos on YouTube," Daily Caller, March 1, 2018, http://dailycaller.com/2018/03/01/splc-youtube-google-trusted-flaggers/.

22. Joe Schoffstall, "Full David Brock Confidential Memo on Fighting Trump," Scribd, https://www.scribd.com/document/337535680/Full-David-Brock-Confidential-Memo-On-Fighting-Trump#from_embed.

Chapter Three: Facebook

1. Andrew Perrin, Monica Anderson, "Share of U.S. Adults Using Social Media, Including Facebook, Is Mostly Unchanged since 2018," Pew Research Center, April 10, 2019, https://www.pewresearch.org/fact-tank/2019/04/10/share-of-u-s-adults-using-social-media-including-facebook-is-mostly-unchanged-since-2018/.

2. Elisa Shearer, Katerina Eva Matsa, "News Use Across Social Media Platforms 2018," Pew Research Center, September 10, 2018, http://www.journalism.org/2018/09/10/news-use-across-social-media-platforms-2018/.

3. Adam Kramer, Jamie Guillory, and Jeffrey Hancock, "Experimental Evidence of Massive-Scale Emotional Contagion through Social Networks," Proceedings of the National Academy of Sciences of the United States of America, June 17, 2014, https://www.pnas.org/content/111/24/8788.full.

4. Robert Booth, "Facebook Reveals News Feed Experiment To Control Emotions," The Guardian, June 29, 2019, https://www.theguardian.com/technology/2014/jun/29/facebook-users-emotions-news-feeds.

5. Gail Sullivan, "Sheryl Sandberg Not Sorry for Facebook Mood Manipulation Study," Washington Post, July 3, 2014, https://www.washingtonpost.com/news/morning-mix/wp/2014/07/03/sheryl-sandberg-not-sorry-for-facebook-mood-manipulation-study/?noredirect=on&utm_term=.61c50fd5dd6f.

6. R. Jai Krishna, "Sandberg: Facebook Study Was 'Poorly Communicated,'" Wall Street Journal, July 2, 2014, https://blogs.wsj.com/digits/2014/07/02/facebooks-sandberg-apologizes-for-news-feed-experiment/?mod=LS1.

7. Michael Nunez, "Former Facebook Workers: We Routinely Suppressed Conservative News," Gizmodo, May 9, 2016, https://gizmodo.com/former-facebook-workers-we-routinely-suppressed-conser-1775461006.

8. Nunez, "Former Facebook Workers."

9. Nunez, "Former Facebook Workers."

10. Kate Conger, Sheera Frenkel, "Dozens at Facebook Unite To Challenge Its 'Intolerant' Liberal Culture," *New York Times*, August 28, 2018, https://www.nytimes.com/2018/08/28/technology/inside-facebook-employees-political-bias.html.

11. Tyler Durden, "Conservative Facebook Employee Who Wrote Memo on 'Intolerant' Liberals Quits," ZeroHedge.com, October 11, 2018, https://www.zerohedge.com/news/2018-10-11/conservative-facebook-employee-who-wrote-memo-intolerant-liberals-quits.

12. Casey Newton, "Facebook Employees Argued Trump's Posts Should Be Banned as Hate Speech," The Verge, October 21, 2016, https://www.theverge.com/2016/10/21/13361908/facebook-employees-trump-ban-hate-speech.

13. Kirsten Grind and Keach Hagey, "Why Did Facebook Fire a Top Executive? Hint: It Had Something To Do with Trump," *Wall Street Journal*, November 11, 2018, https://www.wsj.com/articles/why-did-facebook-fire-a-top-executive-hint-it-had-something-to-do-with-trump-1541965245.

14. Ibid.

15. Ibid.

16. Julie Zhuo (@Julie Zhuo), "I Woke Up at 4am Last Night and Threw Up. I Woke Up This Morning Feeling Groggy and Leaden. I Resisted Checking Facebook for a Few Hours because I Knew the Posts," Facebook post, November 9, 2016, https://www.facebook.com/julie/posts/10102669131580713.

17. Carolyn Everson (@Carolyn Everson), "In My Post Yesterday, I Said We Must Respect the Outcome of the Election and We Need To Begin the Healing Process and Move Forward as a Nation. And I Believe," Facebook post, November 9, 2019, https://www.facebook.com/carolyn.everson/posts/10153941674160913.

18. Mike Isaac, "Rifts Break Open at Facebook Over Kavanaugh Hearing," *New York Times*, October 4, 2018, https://www.nytimes.com/2018/10/04/technology/facebook-kavanaugh-nomination-kaplan.html.

19. Peter Hasson, "Leaked Emails Show Facebook Exec Shared Research with Clinton Campaign," Daily Caller, October 10, 2016, https://dailycaller.

com/2016/10/10/leaked-emails-show-facebook-exec-shared-research-with-clinton-campaign/.

20. Kaitlyn Sullivan (@katersully), "51 People Have Announced Their Support for Kavanaugh. Let's Hold Them ALL Accountable. (Some Are Even Up for Election Next Month!)," Twitter post, October 5, 2018, https://twitter.com/katersully/status/1048348590953906176.

21. Mike McIntire, "How a Putin Fan Overseas Pushed Pro-Trump Propaganda to Americans," *New York Times*, December 17, 2016, https://www.nytimes.com/2016/12/17/world/europe/russia-propaganda-elections.html.

22. Mark Zuckerberg (@Mark Zuckerberg), "I Want To Share Some Thoughts on Facebook and the Election. Our Goal Is To Give Every Person a Voice. We Believe Deeply in People. Assuming That People Understand," Facebook post, November 12, 2016, https://www.facebook.com/zuck/posts/10103253901916271.

23. Josh Constine, "Facebook Now Flags and Down-Ranks Fake news with Help from Outside Face Checkers," TechCrunch.com, December 15, 2016, https://techcrunch.com/2016/12/15/facebook-now-flags-and-down-ranks-fake-news-with-help-from-outside-fact-checkers/.

24. Brendan Nyhan, "Why Fears of Fake News Are Overhyped," Gen. Medium.com, February 4, 2019, https://medium.com/s/reasonable-doubt/why-fears-of-fake-news-are-overhyped-2ed9ca0a52c9.

25. Mark Zuckerberg, "A Blueprint for Content Governance and Enforcement," Notes, Facebook, November 15, 2016, https://www.facebook.com/notes/mark-zuckerberg/a-blueprint-for-content-governance-and-enforcement/10156443129621634/.

26. Jonathan Chait, "Will Trump Be Meeting with His Counterpart—or His Handler?" *New York Magazine*, July 2018, http://nymag.com/intelligencer/2018/07/trump-putin-russia-collusion.html.

27. Sophie Lucido Johnson, "Talking to My Fiancé about My New Girlfriend," *New York Times*, October 12, 2018, https://www.nytimes.com/2018/10/12/style/modern-love-talking-to-my-fiance-about-my-new-girlfriend.html.

28. Josh Constine, "Facebook Will Change Algorithm To Demote 'Borderline Content' That Almost Violates Policies," TechCrunch.com, November 15, 2018, https://techcrunch.com/2018/11/15/facebook-borderline-content/.

29. Peter Hasson, "Facebook Plans To 'Dial Up' Suppression of Certain News Outlets," Daily Caller, May 1, 2018, https://dailycaller.com/2018/05/01/facebook-newsfeed-trusted-sources-dial-up/.

30. "Facebook Engagement Trends in March: The Winners and Losers," Digital Journalism, NewsWhip, https://www.newswhip.com/2018/04/facebook-engagements-march-2018/.

31. Paris Martineau, "Conservative Publishers Hit Hardest by Facebook News Feed Change," The Outline, March 5, 2018, https://theoutline.com/post/3599/conservative-publishers-hit-hardest-by-facebook-news-feed-change?zd=4&zi=6ki6jclk.

32. George Upper and G. S. Hair, "Confirmed: Facebook's Recent Algorithm Change Is Crushing Conservative Sites, Boosting Liberals," Western Journal, March 13, 2018, https://www.westernjournal.com/confirmed-facebooks-recent-algorithm-change-is-crushing-conservative-voices-boosting-liberals/.

33. Oliver Darcy, "Inside the Identity Crisis at the Independent Journal Review, the Outlet That Has Become a Powerhouse in the Trump Era," *Business Insider*, March 21, 2017, https://www.businessinsider.com/independent-journal-review-ijr-identity-trump-2017-3.

34. Joe Concha, "Millennial Conservative Site Lays Off Staff after Facebook Change," *The Hill*, February 16, 2018, https://thehill.com/homenews/media/374195-millennial-conservative-site-lays-off-staff-after-facebook-change.

35. Joe Simonson, "Exclusive: Mass Layoffs at IJR, Leaving Future Uncertain," Daily Caller, February 15, 2018, https://dailycaller.com/2018/02/15/mass-layoffs-ijr/.

36. Matt Naham, "Killed by Facebook," Rare, March 28, 2018, https://web.archive.org/web/20180330051511/https://rare.us/rare-news/the-media/killed-by-facebook-what-its-like-to-work-at-a-website-killed-by-facebook/.

37. Ibid.

38. Hasson, "Facebook Plans To 'Dial Up.'"

39. Deepa Seetharaman, "Facebook's Lonely Conservative Takes on a Power Position," Fox News, https://www.foxnews.com/tech/facebooks-lonely-conservative-takes-on-a-power-position.

40. Ibid.

41. Benjamin Mullin and Sahil Patel, "Facebook Offers News Outlets Millions of Dollars a Year To License Content," *Wall Street Journal*, August 8,

2019, https://www.wsj.com/articles/facebook-offers-news-outlets-millions-of-dollars-a-year-to-license-content-11565294575.

42. Laura Hazard Owen, "Facebook Launches Its 'Test' News Tab in the U.S., but You May Not See It Yet," Nieman Lab, October 25, 2019, https://www.niemanlab.org/2019/10/facebook-launches-its-test-news-tab-in-the-u-s-but-you-may-not-see-it-yet/.

43. Oliver Darcy, "Facebook News Launches with Breitbart as a Source," CNN Business, October 26, 2019, https://www.cnn.com/2019/10/26/media/facebook-news-breitbart/index.html.

44. Noah Shachtman (@NoahShachtman), "Promoting the Political Outfit Which Championed the 'Alt-Right' *Is* Embracing a Political Ideology, Adam," Twitter post, October 26, 2019, https://twitter.com/NoahShachtman/status/1188172308155944961.

45. Charlie Warzel, "Why Will Breitbart Be Included in Facebook News?" *New York Times*, October 25, 2019, https://www.nytimes.com/2019/10/25/opinion/mark-zuckerberg-facebook.html.

46. Joe Marusak, "Facebook Apologizes for Banning Evangelist Franklin Graham for 24 Hours," *Charlotte Observer*, December 29, 2018, https://www.charlotteobserver.com/living/religion/article223714480.html.

47. Ibid.

48. William Davis, "Franklin Graham Claims He Was Banned from Facebook," Daily Caller, December 28, 2018, https://dailycaller.com/2018/12/28/franklin-graham-banned-from-facebook/.

49. Sofia Carbone, "Kassam Banned from Facebook on UK Election Day," HumanEvents.com, May 24, 2019, https://humanevents.com/2019/05/24/kassam-banned-from-facebook-on-uk-election-day/?utm_referrer=https%3A%2F%2Fwww.google.com%2F.

50. Ibid.

51. Mike Brest, "FB Post Honoring Slain Police Officer Labeled as 'Against Our Community Standards,'" Daily Caller, December 31, 2018, https://dailycaller.com/2018/12/31/facebook-police-community-standards-hate/.

52. Ibid.

53. Ginia Bellafante, "Is It Safe To Be Jewish in New York?" *New York Times*, October 31, 2018, https://www.nytimes.com/2018/10/31/nyregion/jewish-bias-safety-nyc.html.

54. Peter Hasson, "Tom Steyer Runs Facebook Ad Comparing President Trump to Saddam Hussein," Daily Caller, October 29, 2018, https://dailycaller.com/2018/10/29/tom-steyer-donald-trump-saddam-hussein/.

55. Peter Hasson, "Democratic Operatives Used Misleading Facebook Pages To Suppress GOP Turnout in Midterms," Daily Caller, January 8, 2019, https://dailycaller.com/2019/01/08/democrat-facebook-campaign-supress/.

56. Richard Nieva, "Facebook's New Rosetta AI System Helps Detect Hate Speech," Cnet.com, September 11, 2018, https://www.cnet.com/news/facebooks-new-rosetta-ai-system-helps-detect-hate-speech/.

57. Ezra Klein "Mark Zuckerberg on Facebook's Hardest year, and What Comes Next," Vox.com, April 2, 2018, https://www.vox.com/2018/4/2/17185052/mark-zuckerberg-facebook-interview-fake-news-bots-cambridge.

58. Tamar Lapin, "Facebook Flagged Declaration of Independence as Hate Speech," *New York Post*, July 5, 2018, https://nypost.com/2018/07/05/facebook-flagged-declaration-of-independence-as-hate-speech/.

59. Rob Price, "Leaked Memo Spells Out Facebook's New 'Ground Rules' Restricting Employee Discussions about Politics and Religion," *Business Insider*, January 20, 2019, https://www.businessinsider.com/facebook-new-rules-employee-discussions-politics-bullying-religion-2019-1.

60. Chris White, "Report: Facebook's New Rules Ban Employees from Changing Collegues' Minds," Daily Caller, January 15, 2019, https://dailycaller.com/2019/01/15/facebook-censorship-internal-memo/.

61. "About," Facebook, https://newsroom.fb.com/company-info/.

Chapter Four: One Nation under Google

1. Jeff Desjardins, "How Google Retains More Than 90% of Market Share," *Business Insider*, April 23, 2018, https://www.businessinsider.com/how-google-retains-more-than-90-of-market-share-2018-4.

2. Clare Carr, "Discover.google.com Gone as a Referring URL in Latest Referral Traffic Trends," Parse.ly, January 7, 2019, https://blog.parse.ly/post/8225/december-2018-referral-traffic-trends-google-discover-googleapis/.

3. Tristan Harris, "How a Handful of Tech Companies Control Billions of Minds Every Day," TED Talk, April 2017, https://www.ted.com/talks/tristan_harris_the_manipulative_tricks_tech_companies_use_to_capture_your_attention?language=en.

4. Robert Epstein, Roger Mohr Jr., and Jeremy Martinez, "The Search Suggestion Effect (SSE): How Search Suggestions Can Be Used TO Shift Opinions and Voting Preferences Dramatically and without People's Awareness," American

Institute for Behavioral Research and Technology, April 26, 2018, http://aibrt. org/downloads/EPSTEIN_MOHR_&_MARTINEZ_2018-WPA-The_Search_Suggestion_Effect-SSE-WP-17-03.pdf.

5.   Damore et al. v. Google, 18CV321529, (Superior Court of California, Santa Clara, April 18, 2018) https://www.dhillonlaw.com/wp-content/uploads/2018/04/20180418-Damore-et-al.-v.-Google-FAC_Endorsed.pdf.

6.   Ibid.

7.   Althea Nagai, "The Implicit Association Test: Flawed Science Tricks Americans into Believing They Are Unconscious Racists," Special Report No. 196, Heritage Foundation, December 12, 2017, https://www.heritage. org/sites/default/files/2017-12/SR-196.pdf.

8.   Julia Belluz, "Companies like Starbucks Love Anti-Bias Training. But It Doesn't Work—and May Backfire," Vox, May 29, 2018, https://www.vox.com/science-and-health/2018/4/19/17251752/philadelphia-starbucks-arrest-racial-bias-training.

9.   "Bias Busting @ Work Slides," Ada Initiatives, October 20, 2015, https://docs.google.com/presentation/d/1RJorJs1sClLKHD4dqgrxOBXn-hhIyOXLu2k8zfHatwA/edit#slide=id.g1db96eec6_074.

10. Damore et al. v. Google, 18CV321529.

11. Ibid.

12. Ibid.

13. Ibid.

14. Google Workers for Action on Climate, "Open Letter on Climate Action at Google," Medium.com, November 4, 2019, https://medium.com/@googworkersac/ruth-porat-497bbb841b52.

15. J. Arthur Bloom, "Inside Google's Microaggressions Newsletter: Pronoun Problems, Soy Police, and a Deaf Person Told To Watch Her Tone," Daily Caller, June 25, 2019, https://dailycaller.com/2019/06/25/inside-google-microaggressions-newsletter/.

16. Damore et al. v. Google, 18CV321529.

17. Chris White, "Google Leadership Reacting to Trump's Victory," Daily Caller, September 13, 2018, https://dailycaller.com/2018/09/13/google-trump-election-video-sergey-brin/.

18. Allum Bokhari, "Leaked Video: Google Leadership's Dismayed Reaction to Trump Election," Breitbart, September

12, 2018, https://www.breitbart.com/tech/2018/09/12/
leaked-video-google-leaderships-dismayed-reaction-to-trump-election/.

19. Benjamin Chapman, Paul Duberstein, Slivia Sörensen, and Jeffrey Lyness, "Gender Differences in Five Factor Model Personality Traits in an Elderly Cohort: Extension of Robuset and Surprising Findings to an Older Generation," *PubMed Central*, 43(06) (October 2007): 1594–1603, https://www.ncbi.nlm.nih.gov/pmc/articles/PMC2031866/.

20. Peter Hasson, "Anti-Conservative Censorship Spreads from Campuses to Big Tech," Daily Caller, January 10, 2018, https://dailycaller.com/2018/01/10/anti-conservative-censorship-spreads-from-campuses-to-big-tech/.

21. *Damore et al. v. Google*, 18CV321529.

22. Ibid.

23. Ibid.

24. Meghan Fischer, Garrett Johnson, and Aaron Ginn, "Viewpoint Diversity in Tech: Reality or Myth?" Lincoln Network, January 6, 2018, https://joinlincoln.org/viewpoint-diversity.

25. Ibid.

26. *Damore et al. v. Google*, 18CV321529.

27. Ibid.

28. Allum Bokhari, "'The Good Censor': Leaked Google Briefing Admits Abandonment of Free Speech for 'Safety and Civility,'" Breitbart, October 9, 2018, https://www.breitbart.com/tech/2018/10/09/the-good-censor-leaked-google-briefing-admits-abandonment-of-free-speech-for-safety-and-civility/.

29. Allum Bokhari, "The Good Censor—Google Leak," Sribd.com, March 2018, https://www.scribd.com/document/390521673/The-Good-Censor-GOOGLE-LEAK.

30. John McKinnon and Douglas MacMillan, "Google Workers Discussed Tweaking Search Function To Counter Travel Ban," *Wall Street Journal*, September 20, 2018, https://www.wsj.com/articles/google-workers-discussed-tweaking-search-function-to-counter-travel-ban-1537488472.

31. Allum Bokhari, "Exclusive: Leftist Google Employees Conspire To Undermine Breitbart's Ad Revenue," Breitbart, February 13, 2018, https://www.breitbart.com/tech/2018/02/13/exclusive-google-employees-are-trying-to-pull-ad-revenue-from-breitbart-news/.

32. Aaron Clifford, "3 Ways To Improve Your Google Search Rankings," AdWeek, February 4, 2019, https://www.adweek.com/digital/3-ways-to-improve-your-google-search-rankings/.

33. "Building a Better News Experience on YouTube, Together," Official Blog, YouTube, July 9, 2018, https://youtube.googleblog.com/2018/07/building-better-news-experience-on.html.

34. Peter Hasson, "Jimmy Kimmel Absolutely Butchers Gay Wedding Cake Ruling and It's Not Even Close," Daily Caller, February 9, 2018, https://dailycaller.com/2018/02/09/jimmy-kimmel-absolutely-butchers-gay-wedding-cake-ruling-and-its-not-even-close-video/.

35. "'Gay Wedding Cake' YouTube Search Results" Page 1, YouTube, January 30, 2019, https://www.youtube.com/results?sp=CAA%253D&search_query=gay+wedding+cake.

36. Steven Crowder, "HIDDEN CAM: #GayWeddingCakes at Muslim Bakeries?" YouTube, April 2, 2015, https://www.youtube.com/watch?v=RgWIhYAtan4.

37. Michelle Cretella, "I'm a Pediatrician. Here's What I Did When a Little Boy Patient Said He Was a Girl," Daily Caller, December 11, 2017, https://www.dailysignal.com/2017/12/11/cretella-transcript/.

38. Katrina Trinko, "YouTube Won't Let a Medical Doctor Say This Sentence," Daily Signal, November 5, 2019, https://www.dailysignal.com/2019/11/05/youtube-wont-let-a-medical-doctor-say-this-sentence/.

39. "Continuing Our Work To Improve Recommendations on YouTube," Official Blog, YouTube, January 25, 2019, https://youtube.googleblog.com/2019/01/continuing-our-work-to-improve.html.

40. Casey Newton, "YouTube Says It Will Recommend Fewer Videos about Conspiracy Theories," The Verge, January 25, 2019, https://www.theverge.com/2019/1/25/18197301/youtube-algorithm-conspiracy-theories-misinformation.

41. Grant Eizikowitz, "How To Get a Billion Views on YouTube," Business Insider, April 20, 2018, https://www.businessinsider.com/how-to-get-billion-views-viral-hit-youtube-2018-4.

42. Peter Hasson, "YouTube To Step Up Suppression of Videos That Don't Violate Any Rules, Promote News Outlets," Daily Caller, June 5, 2019, https://dailycaller.com/2019/06/05/youtube-suppress-borderline-videos-promote-news/.

43. Ian Miles Cheong, "Conservative and Independent YouTube Channels Hit by Censorship and Demonetization," Daily Caller, August 11, 2017, https://dailycaller.com/2017/08/11/conservative-and-independent-youtube-channels-hit-by-censorship-and-demonetization/.

44. Ian Miles Cheong, "YouTube Demonetizes Small Channels with New Partnership Policy," Daily Caller, January 17, 2018, https://dailycaller.com/2018/01/17/youtube-demonetizes-small-channels-with-new-partnership-policy/.

45. Eric Lieberman, "Google's Fake News 'Fact Checkers' Include Snopes, Politifact," Daily Caller, April 7, 2017, https://dailycaller.com/2017/04/07/googles-fake-news-fact-checkers-include-snopes-politifact/.

46. Ibid.

47. Peter Hasson, "Exclusive: Google Employees Debated Burying Conservative Media in Search," Daily Caller, November 29, 2018, https://dailycaller.com/2018/11/29/google-censorship-conservative-media/.

48. Alexi Mostous, "Google Faces Questions over Videos on YouTube," The Times, February 9, 2017, https://www.thetimes.co.uk/article/google-faces-questions-over-videos-on-youtube-3km257v8d.

49. Olivia Solon, "Google's Bad Week: YouTube Loses Millions as Advertising Row Reaches US," The Guardian, March 25, 2017, https://www.theguardian.com/technology/2017/mar/25/google-youtube-advertising-extremist-content-att-verizon.

50. Peter Hasson, "Google Has an Actual Secret Speech Police," Daily Caller, January 19, 2018, https://dailycaller.com/2018/01/19/google-youtube-censorship-demonetize-hate-speech/.

51. Levi Sumagaysay, "Facebook, Google, Twitter Could Lose Unilever Ads," Mercury News, February 12, 2018, https://www.mercurynews.com/2018/02/12/facebook-google-twitter-could-lose-unilever-ads/.

52. Mark Bergen, "YouTube's New Moderators Mistakenly Pull Right-Wing Channels," Bloomberg, February 28, 2018, https://www.bloomberg.com/news/articles/2018-02-28/youtube-s-new-moderators-mistakenly-pull-right-wing-channels.

53. Peter Hasson, "YouTube's Algorithms Continue Snaring Critics of Political Correctness," Daily Caller, February 1, 2018, https://dailycaller.com/2018/02/01/youtube-algorithm-dave-rubin-jordan-peterson-demonetize/.

54. Peter Hasson, "YouTube Sponsoring 9/11 Truther as Part of Multimillion Dollar Diversity Program," Daily Caller, March 4, 2018, http://dailycaller.com/2018/03/04/youtube-9-11-truther/.

Chapter Five: Twitter's Free Speech Farce

1. "Q4 and Fiscal Year 2018 Letter to Shareholders," Twitter, February 7, 2019, Twitter, https://s22.q4cdn.com/826641620/files/doc_financials/2018/q4/Q4-2018-Shareholder-Letter.pdf.

2. Michael Gove, "Donald Trump Interview: Brexit Will Be a Great Thing," *The Times,* January 15, 2017, https://www.thetimes.co.uk/edition/news/donald-trump-interview-brexit-britain-trade-deal-europe-queen-5m0bc2tns.

3. Kelsey Lucas, "Meet the Serial Killer Who Murdered Living Babies," Daily Signal, May 4, 2014, https://www.dailysignal.com/2014/05/04/meet-serial-killer-murdered-100-living-babies/.

4. Matthew Archbold, "Why Did Gosnell Sever the Babies' Spinal Cord If They Were Already Dead?" *National Catholic Register,* April 23, 2013, http://www.ncregister.com/blog/matthew-archbold/why-did-gosnell-sever-the-babies-spinal-cord-if-they-were-already-dead.

5. Charlie Spiering, "58 Horrific Details from the Kermit Gosnell Trial That You Do Not Want To Read," *Washington Examiner,* April 18, 2013, https://www.washingtonexaminer.com/58-horrific-details-from-the-kermit-gosnell-trial-that-you-do-not-want-to-read.

6. Ibid.

7. Ibid.

8. Ibid.

9. Ibid.

10. David Weigel, "A Jury of Your Peers," Slate, April 15, 2013, https://slate.com/news-and-politics/2013/04/kermit-gosnell-abortion-trial-conservatives-took-to-twitter-to-shame-mainstream-media-into-covering-the-philadelphia-abortion-clinic-trial.html.

11. Rani Molla, "Tech Employees Are Much More Liberal Than Their Employers—at Least as Far as the Candidates They Support," Vox, October 31, 2018, https://www.recode.net/2018/10/31/18039528/tech-employees-politics-liberal-employers-candidates.

12. Casey Newton, "Inside Twitter, Employees Reckon with Trump," The Verge, January 12, 2017, https://www.theverge.com/2017/1/12/14256818/donald-trump-twitter-ban-employee-reaction.

13. Ibid.

14. Peter Leyden, "The Great Lesson of California in America's New Civil War," Medium, January 19, 2018, https://medium.com/s/state-of-the-future/the-great-lesson-of-california-in-americas-new-civil-war-e52e2861f30.

15. Peter Hasson, "Twitter CEO Caves to Liberal Backlash, Says He Was Wrong To Eat Chick-fil-A," Daily Caller, June 10, 2018, https://dailycaller.com/2018/06/10/twitter-ceo-chick-fil-a-gay-marriage/.

16. "Statement of Nick Pickles Before the Committee on the Judiciary," U.S. House of Representatives, July 17, 2018, https://docs.house.gov/meetings/JU/JU00/20180717/108546/HHRG-115-JU00-Wstate-PicklesN-20180717.pdf.

17. Dan Gainor, "Twitter CEO Dorsey: Comment Backing 'Free Speech' Was 'a Joke,'" NewsBusters, October 16, 2018, https://www.newsbusters.org/blogs/techwatch/dan-gainor/2018/10/16/twitter-ceo-dorsey-comment-backing-free-speech-was-joke.

18. Paul Bedard, "Twitter Exec: 'Jail,' 'Impeachment' for Trump, Calls Social Media Chief 'Racist D—k,'" *Washington Examiner,* July 15, 2019, https://www.washingtonexaminer.com/washington-secrets/twitter-exec-jail-impeachment-for-trump-calls-social-media-chief-racist-d.

19. "Me. We. Us. The World. #GrowTogether," Company, Twitter, September 2017, https://about.twitter.com/en_us/company/our-culture.html.

20. Avery Anapol, "Twitter Employee Who Deleted Trump's Account Reveals Himself," *The Hill,* November 29, 2017, https://thehill.com/homenews/administration/362468-twitter-employee-who-deleted-trumps-account-reveals-himself.

21. Jamie Weinstein, "White Nationalism Leader Richard Spencer Defends Meager Conference Attendance Compared to Bronycon," Daily Caller, November 24, 2016, https://dailycaller.com/2016/11/24/white-nationalist-leader-richard-spencer-defends-meager-conference-attendance-compared-to-bronycon/.

22. Joseph Wulfsohn, "Ben Shapiro Shames *The Economist* after Referring to Him as 'Alt-Right': 'That's a Vile Lie,'" Fox News, March 29, 2019, https://

www.foxnews.com/entertainment/ben-shapiro-shames-the-economist-into-changing-headline-after-referring-to-him-as-alt-right.

23. Jack Dorsey (@jack), "We're Committing Twitter To Help Increase the Collective Health, Openness, and Civility of Public Conversation, and To Hold Ourselves Publicly Accountable," Twitter post, March 1, 2018, https://twitter.com/jack/status/969234275420655616.

24. Ibid.

25. "Statement of Nick Pickles Before the Committee on the Judiciary," U.S. House of Representatives, July 17, 2018, https://docs.house.gov/meetings/JU/JU00/20180717/108546/HHRG-115-JU00-Wstate-PicklesN-20180717.pdf.

26. Alex Thompson, "Twitter Appears To Have Fixed 'Shadow Ban' of Prominent Republicans like the RNC Chair and Trump Jr.'s Spokesman," Vice News, July 25, 2018, https://news.vice.com/en_us/article/43paqq/twitter-is-shadow-banning-prominent-republicans-like-the-rnc-chair-and-trump-jrs-spokesman.

27. Peter Hasson (@peterjhasson), "In This Interview with @guypbenson (Who Asked All the Right Questions), @jack Accurately Notes That Twitter Shifted to a Ranked Timeline Two Years (Left)," Twitter post, August 2, 2018, https://twitter.com/peterjhasson/status/1025377568676036608.

28. Vijaya Gadde and David Gasca, "Measuring Healthy Conversation," Company, Twitter, July 30, 2018, https://blog.twitter.com/official/en_us/topics/company/2018/measuring_healthy_conversation.html.

29. Gadde and Gasca, "Measuring Healthy Conversation."

30. Peter Hasson, "Twitter Plans 'Hate Speech' Crackdown after Backlash from Upset Employees," Daily Caller, August 8, 2018, https://dailycaller.com/2018/08/08/twitter-jack-dorsey-hate-speech-policy/.

31. Ibid.

32. "Man," Dictionary, Merriam Webster, https://www.merriam-webster.com/dictionary/man

33. "Woman," Dictionary, Merriam Webster, https://www.merriam-webster.com/dictionary/woman.

34. Daniella Greenbaum, "Here Is the Column That Business Insider Spiked," Washington Examiner, July 11, 2018, https://www.weeklystandard.com/daniella-greenbaum/

here-is-the-column-about-scarjo-that-business-insider-spiked-to-appease-a-social-justice-mob.

35. Joe Simonson, *Business Insider* Takes Down Conservative Column after Employees Revolt," Daily Caller, July 10, 2018, https://dailycaller.com/2018/07/10/business-insider-column-revolt/.

36. Peter Hasson and Henry Rodgers, "Ilhan Omar Urges Kieth Ellison To Investigate USA Powerlifting for Barring Biological Males from Women's Events," Daily Caller, February 6, 2019, https://dailycaller.com/2019/02/06/ilhan-omar-transgender-powerlifting/.

37. Peter Hasson, "Democrats Unanimous as House Passes Bill Forcing Schools To Let Male Athletes Compete in Girls' Sports," Daily Caller, May 17, 2019, https://dailycaller.com/2019/05/17/house-equality-act-transgender-womens-sports/.

38. Peter Hasson, "Every Democratic 2020 Frontrunner Supports Bill Forcing Male Athletes into Girls' Sports," Daily Caller, June 18, 2019, https://dailycaller.com/2019/06/18/2020-democrats-transgender-athletes-equality-act/.

39. Meghan Murphy, "Twitter Wants Me To Shut Up and the Right Wants Me To Join Them; I Don't Think I Should Have To Do Either," Feminist Current, November 20, 2018, https://www.feministcurrent.com/2018/11/20/twitter-wants-shut-right-wants-join-dont-think-either/.

40. Vijaya Gadde and Del Harvey, "Creating New Policies Together," Company, Twitter, September 25, 2018, https://blog.twitter.com/official/en_us/topics/company/2018/Creating-new-policies-together.html.

41. Louise Matsakis, "Twitter Releases New Policy on 'Dehumanizing Speech,'" Wired, September 25, 2018, https://www.wired.com/story/twitter-dehumanizing-speech-policy/.

42. Rachel Stoltzofoos, "Twitter Suspends Another Porminent User for Stating Basic Truths about Transgenderism," Daily Caller, May 17, 2019, https://dailycaller.com/2019/05/17/twitter-suspends-transgenderism/.

43. Ibid.

44. Niel Munro, "Twitter Blacklists Famed Gender Dysphoria Researcher Ray Blanchard," Breitbart, May 13, 2019, https://www.breitbart.com/politics/2019/05/13/twitter-blacklists-famed-gender-dysphoria-researcher-ray-blanchard/.

45. "Pope Francis: It's 'Terrible' Children Taught They Can Choose Gender," *Catholic Herald*, August 3, 2016, https://catholicherald.co.uk/news/2016/08/03/pope-francis-its-terrible-children-taught-they-can-choose-gender/.

46. Ibid.

47. Amber Athey, "Two Conservatives Suspended from Twitter—One for Tweeting about Brussels Sprouts," Daily Caller, January 3, 2019, https://dailycaller.com/2019/01/03/newsbusters-daily-wire-conservative-suspended-twitter-brussels-sprouts/.

48. Amber Athey, "Twitter Restores Popular Beto O'Rourke Parody Account," Daily Caller, January 23, 2019, https://dailycaller.com/2019/01/23/twitter-beto-orourke-parody-suspended/.

49. Ibid.

50. Eric Lieberman, "Twitter: 'Our Mistake' for Restricting User Who Criticized Hamas," Daily Caller, May 28, 2018, https://dailycaller.com/2018/05/28/twitter-restricts-user-who-criticized-hamas/.

51. Neetu Chandak, "Twitter bans Center for Immigration Studies from Promoting Tweets about Illegal Aliens," Daily Caller, September 12, 2018, https://dailycaller.com/2018/09/12/twitter-center-immigration-studies-illegal-aliens/.

52. Andy Lassner (@andylassner), "Oh for God's Sake. I'm as Liberal as They Come. Jesse Is a Harmless Guy Who Happens To Be Funny as Hell, Not To Mention My Friend. He Did Everything with a Wink on Here. If Twitter Really Banned Him, That's Just Stupid," Twitter post, November 25, 2018, https://web.archive.org/web/20181126004716/https:/twitter.com/andylassner/status/1066852756533604352.

53. Ben Sasse (@BenSasse), "Jesse Kelly Can't Stand Me. And I Think His Tribal War Scalping Stuff Is Stupid and Wrong. But That Doesn't Matter Much Compared to the Bigger Picture Here," Twitter post, November 26, 2018, https://twitter.com/BenSasse/status/1067159950949056513.

54. Jesse Kelly, "Twitter Banned Me for Literally No Reason, But in the End They'll Lose," The Federalist, November 26, 2018, http://thefederalist.com/2018/11/26/twitter-banned-literally-no-reason-end-theyll-lose/.

55. Amber Athey, "Daily Caller Editor in Chief Locked Out of Account for Tweeting 'Learn To Code,'" Daily Caller, February 6, 2019, https://dailycaller.com/2019/02/06/daily-caller-twitter-locked-learn-to-code/.

56. Ibid.

57. Peter Hasson, "Twitter: Saying Dana Loesch's Kids Need To Be Murdered Does Not Violate Rules," Daily Caller, August 27, 2018, https://dailycaller.com/2018/08/27/dana-loesch-twitter-death-threats/.

58. Peter Hasson, "Twitter Reverses Ruling after Backlash, Concedes It's against the Rules To Wish Death upon Dana Loesch's Children," Daily Caller, August 27, 2018, https://dailycaller.com/2018/08/27/dana-loesch-twitter-death-threats-reversed/.

59. "Meghan McCain's Husband Slams Twitter for Waiting Hours To Remove Tweet Threatening Wife," CBS News, September 1, 2018, https://www.cbsnews.com/news/ben-domenech-meghan-mccain-slams-twitter-for-waiting-hours-to-remove-threatening-tweet/.

60. Maureen Groppe, "Twitter Apologizes to Meghan McCain for Not Acting Faster To Remove a Doctored Photo Showing Gun Pointed at Her," USA Today, September 5, 2018, https://www.usatoday.com/story/news/politics/2018/09/05/twitter-apologizes-meghan-mccain-not-removing-photo-faster/1205340002/.

61. Ben Domenech, "Twitter CEO Jack Dorsey Lied under Oath to Congress. Shouldn't That Matter?" The Federalist, November 26, 2018, https://thefederalist.com/2018/11/26/jack-dorsey-lied-under-oath-to-congress-shouldnt-that-matter/.

62. Selina Wang, "Twitter Delves Deeper into News Curation," Mercury News, June 13, 2018, https://www.mercurynews.com/2018/06/13/twitter-delves-deeper-into-news-curation/.

63. "Job Posting," Careers, Twitter, January 20, 2019, https://careers.twitter.com/content/careers-twitter/en/jobs-search.html?q=journalist&team=&location=.

64. "Student Says He Was Trying To Defuse Situation after Staredown with Native American Elder Goes Viral," Moments, Twitter, January 21, 2019, https://twitter.com/i/moments/1086718692270972929.

Chapter Six: Purging Pro-Lifers

1. Robert George, "Undergraduates Say the Darndest Things. When Discussing the History of Racial Injustice, I Frequently Ask Them What Their Position on Slavery Would Have Been," Facebook post, Facebook, April 28, 2016, https://www.facebook.com/robert.p.george.39/posts/10208487901087703.

2. Lydia Saad, "Trimesters Still Key to U.S. Abortion Views," Gallup News, June13, 2018, https://news.gallup.com/poll/235469/trimesters-key-abortion-views.aspx.

3. "Americans' Opinions on Abortion," Knights of Columbus and the Marist College Institute for Public Opinion, January 2018, http://kofc.org/un/en/resources/communications/abortion-limits-favored.pdf.

4. "Abortion," In Depth: Topics A to Z, Gallup, May 2019, https://news.gallup.com/poll/1576/abortion.aspx.

5. "Pregnancy Week by Week," Healthy Lifestyle Mayo Clinic, July 12, 2017, https://www.mayoclinic.org/healthy-lifestyle/pregnancy-week-by-week/in-depth/prenatal-care/art-20045302.

6. "Fetal Growth and Development," South Dakota Department of Health, 1995, https://doh.sd.gov/abortion/assets/fetal.pdf.

7. "Planned Parenthood," Influence and Lobbying Organizations, OpenSecrets.org, 2018, https://www.opensecrets.org/orgs/summary.php?id=D000000591&cycle=2018.

8. Ibid.

9. Peter Hasson, "Democratic Platform Calls for Taxpayer-Funded Abortions," Daily Caller, June 26, 2016, https://dailycaller.com/2016/06/26/democratic-platform-calls-for-taxpayer-funded-abortions/.

10. Ibid.

11. Peter Hasson, "Seven Louis Farrakhan Quotes on Jews, Gays, and White People," Daily Caller, January 26, 2018, https://dailycaller.com/2018/01/26/louis-farrakhan-barack-obama-nation-of-islam/.

12. Peter Hasson, "Women's March Flies into Damage Control over Farrakhan Ties," Daily Caller, March 6, 2018, https://dailycaller.com/2018/03/06/womens-march-tamika-mallory-defends-louis-farrakhan-ties/.

13. Leah McSweeney and Jacob Siegel, "Is the Women's March Melting Down?" Tablet Magazine, December 10, 2018, https://www.tabletmag.com/jewish-news-and-politics/276694/is-the-womens-march-melting-down.

14. Ibid.

15. Jackie Kucinich, "Southern Poverty Law Center Quietly Joins the Roster of Big Groups Walking Away from the Women's March," Daily Beast, January 11, 2019, https://www.thedailybeast.com/

southern-poverty-law-center-quietly-joins-the-roster-of-big-groups-walking-away-from-the-womens-march.

16. Rossalyn Warren, "Facebook Is Ignoring Anti-Abortion Fake News," *New York Times,* November 10, 2017, https://www.nytimes.com/2017/11/10/opinion/facebook-fake-news-abortion.html.

17. Ibid.

18. Jessica Valenti (@JessicaValenti), "Whoever Edited That Atlantic Piece on 'Late-Term Abortions' Should Be Embarrassed," Twitter post, Twitter, February 4, 2019, https://web.archive.org/save/https://twitter.com/JessicaValenti/status/1092477342855938049.

19. Kirstin Palovick, "'ThriVe Lies': Why Pro-Choice Activists Rallied outside a St. Louis Anti-Abortion Clinic," Rewire. News, February 13, 2017, https://rewire.news/article/2017/02/13/thrive-lies-pro-choice-activists-rallied-outside-st-louis-anti-abortion-clinic/.

20. Peter Hasson, "Pennsylvania Democrat Brian Sims Slammed for Non-Apology Attacking Pro-Lifers," Daily Caller, May 8, 2019, https://dailycaller.com/2019/05/08/pennsylvania-brian-sims-pro-life/.

21. Sean Davis, "Now We Know Why Reporters Won't Cover the Planned Parenthood Videos," The Federalist, August 20, 2015, https://thefederalist.com/2015/08/20/now-we-know-why-reporters-wont-cover-the-planned-parenthood-videos/.

22. April Glaser, "YouTube's Search Results for 'Abortion' Show Exactly What Anti-Abortion Activists Want Women To See," Slate, December 21, 2018, https://slate.com/technology/2018/12/youtube-search-abortion-results-pro-life.html.

23. Ibid.

24. Allum Bokhari, "'The Smoking Gun': Google Manipulated YouTube Search Results for Abortion, Maxine Waters, David Hogg," Breitbart, January 16, 2019, https://www.breitbart.com/tech/2019/01/16/google-youtube-search-blacklist-smoking-gun/.

25. Allum Bokhari, "YouTube Admits It Meddled with Abortion Search Results—But Calls Downranked Videos 'Misinformation,'" Breitbart, January 17, 2019, https://www.breitbart.com/tech/2019/01/17/youtube-admits-it-meddled-with-abortion-search-results-but-calls-downranked-videos-misinformation/.

26. Ibid.

27. "William Wilberforce," Religions, BBC, July 5, 2011, http://www.bbc. co.uk/religion/religions/christianity/people/williamwilberforce_1.shtml.

28. "About Susan B. Anthony List," About, SBA-List.org, https://www.sba-list. org/about-susan-b-anthony-list.

29. Ibid.

30. Mallory Quigley, "Facebook STILL Censoring Pro-Life Ads," Press Releases, SBA-List.org, November 1, 2018, https://www.sba-list.org/ newsroom/press-releases/facebook-still-censoring-pro-life-ads.

31. Becket Adams, "Facebook Censoring Pro-Life Political Ads, Again," *Washington Examiner,* November 1, 2018, https://www.washingtonexaminer.com/opinion/ facebook-censoring-pro-life-political-ads-again.

32. Steven Ertelt, "Twitter Censors Pro-Life Group: No Advertiser Is Permitted To Use the Phrase 'Killing Babies,'" LifeNews.com, October 24, 2017, https://www.lifenews.com/2017/10/24/twitter-censors-pro-life-group-no-advertiser-is-permitted-to-use-the-phrase-killing-babies/.

33. Ibid.

34. Andy Biggs, "Blocked: How the Pro-Life Movement Is Being Censored on Social Media," *The Hill,* January 24, 2018, https://thehill.com/blogs/ congress-blog/technology/370455-blocked-how-the-pro-life-movement-is-being-censored-on-social.

35. Susan Berry, "Facebook Blocks Crowdfunding Site for 'Roe v. Wade' Movie," Breitbart, January 11, 2018, https://www.breitbart.com/entertainment/2018/01/11/ nick-loeb-producing-roe-v-wade-movie-crowdfund-site-blocked-facebook/.

36. Ibid.

37. Becket Adams, "Facebook Censoring Pro-Life Political Ads, Again," *Washington Examiner,* November 1, 2018, https://www.washingtonexaminer.com/opinion/ facebook-censoring-pro-life-political-ads-again.

38. "Twitter: Stop Aiding Pro-Life Lies," Petitions, ReproAction, https:// actionnetwork.org/petitions/twitter-stop-aiding-pro-life-lies/.

39. Mary Margaret Olohan, "In Check on Live Action, Fact Checkers Cited Doctor Who Openly Spewed Hate for Anti-Abortion Groups," Daily Caller, September 19, 2019, https://dailycaller.com/2019/09/19/ live-action-fact-check-biased/.

40. Ibid.

41. Mary Margaret Olohan, "Fact Check of Live Action Content 'Fell Short' of International Fact Checking Network Standards," Daily Caller, September 27, 2019, https://dailycaller.com/2019/09/27/live-actions-fact-checkers-abortion/.

42. "2016–2017 Annual Report," Planned Parenthood, December 29, 2017, https://www.plannedparenthood.org/uploads/filer_public/d4/50/d450c016-a6a9-4455-bf7f-711067db5ff7/20171229_ar16-17_p01_lowres.pdf.

43. Sara Ashley O'Brien, "Sheryl Sandberg Gives $1 Million to Planned Parenthood," CNN Business, February 1, 2017, https://money.cnn.com/2017/02/01/technology/sheryl-sandberg-planned-parenthood/index.html.

44. Marina Fang, "Sheryl Sandberg Donates $1 Million to Planned Parenthood's Advocacy Efforts," HuffPost, June 28, 2019, https://www.huffpost.com/entry/sheryl-sandberg-planned-parenthood-donation-abortion-laws_n_5d151134e4b07f6ca57a55c1.

45. "Return of Exempt Organization Public Disclosure Copy," Silicon Valley Community Foundation, December 31, 2017, https://www.siliconvalleycf.org/sites/default/files/documents/financial/2017-irs-form-990.pdf.

Chapter Seven: Speech Police

1. Abha Bhattarai, "Breitbart Lost 90% of Its Advertisers in Two Months: Who's Still There?" *Washington Post,* June 8, 2017, https://www.washingtonpost.com/news/business/wp/2017/06/08/breitbart-lost-90-percent-of-its-advertisers-in-two-months-whos-still-there/

2. Adam Raymond, "Robert Mercer, Billionaire Bannon Booster, Quits Hedge Fund, Sells Breitbart Stake," *New York Magazine,* November 2, 2017, http://nymag.com/intelligencer/2017/11/robert-mercer-quits-hedge-fund-sells-breitbart-stake.html.

3. Peter Hasson, "Sleeping Giants' Anonymous Founder Unmasked; Top Ad Writer behind Boycott Campaign Targeting Breitbart, Ingraham," Daily Caller, July 16, 2018, https://dailycaller.com/2018/07/16/sleeping-giants-founder-rivitz/.

4. Chuck Ross, "David Brock Finally Apologizes to Bernie Sanders in Desperate Open Letter," Daily Caller,

January 10, 2017, https://dailycaller.com/2017/01/10/
david-brock-finally-apologizes-to-bernie-sanders-in-desperate-open-letter/.

5. Tyler O'Neil, "SPLC's 'Hate Group' Accusation Outed as a Scam, More
Than 60 Groups Considering Lawsuits," PJMedia, April 10, 2019, https://
pjmedia.com/trending/splcs-hate-group-accusation-outed-as-a-scam-more-
than-60-groups-considering-lawsuits/.

6. Ben Schreckinger, "Has a Civil Rights Stalwart Lost
Its Way?" *Politico Magazine,* July/August 2017, https://
www.politico.com/magazine/story/2017/06/28/
morris-dees-splc-trump-southern-poverty-law-center-215312.

7. Pau Bedard, "Support for Southern Poverty Law Center Links Scalise,
Family Research Council Shooters," *Washington Examiner,* June 14, 2017,
https://www.washingtonexaminer.com/support-for-southern-poverty-law-
center-links-scalise-family-research-council-shooters.

8. Peter Hasson, "SPLC Pulls Controversial 'Anti-Muslim Extremist' List
after Legal Threats," Daily Caller, April 19, 2018, https://dailycaller.
com/2018/04/19/splc-maajid-nawaz-muslim-extremist/.

9. Ayaan Hirsi Ali, "Why Is the Southern Poverty Law Center Targeting
Liberals?" *New York Times,* August 24, 2017, https://www.nytimes.
com/2017/08/24/opinion/southern-poverty-law-center-liberals-islam.html.

10. Joe Schoffstall, "Southern Poverty Law Center Has More Than $90
Million in Offshore Funds," Free Beacon, June 20, 2018, https://freebeacon.
com/politics/southern-poverty-law-center-90-million-offshore-funds/.

11. Adam Rubenstein, "SPLC Targets Feminist Scholar Christina
Hoff Sommers," Archives, *Weekly Standard*, February 27,
2018, https://www.weeklystandard.com/adam-rubenstein/
splc-targets-feminist-scholar-christina-hoff-sommers.

12. Ibid.

13. Chuck Ross, "Southern Poverty Law Center Apologizes to Ben Carson
for Putting Him on Its 'Extremist' List," Daily Caller, February 11, 2015,
https://dailycaller.com/2015/02/11/southern-poverty-law-center-apologizes-
to-ben-carson-for-putting-him-on-its-extremist-list/.

14. "16 Things To Know about…Ben Carson," Blog, PBS, https://www.pbs.
org/weta/washingtonweek/blog-post/16-things-know-about-ben-carson.

15. Chuck Ross, "Southern Poverty Law Center Apologizes to Ben Carson
for Putting Him on Its 'Extremist' List," Daily Caller, February 11, 2015,

https://dailycaller.com/2015/02/11/southern-poverty-law-center-apologizes-to-ben-carson-for-putting-him-on-its-extremist-list/.

16. Peter Hasson, "SPLC President Richard Cohen Resigns from Embattled Left-Wing Nonprofit," Daily Caller, March 22, 2019, https://dailycaller.com/2019/03/22/splc-richard-cohen-resigns/. Peter Hasson, "'Highly Profitable Scam': Southern Poverty Law Center 'Ripping Off Donors,' Former Staffer Says," Daily Caller, March 21, 2019, https://dailycaller.com/2019/03/21/southern-poverty-law-center-scam-morris-dees/.

17. Bob Moser, "The Reckoning of Morris Dees and the Southern Poverty Law Center," New Yorker, March 21, 2019, https://www.newyorker.com/news/news-desk/the-reckoning-of-morris-dees-and-the-southern-poverty-law-center.

18. Bob Moser, "The Reckoning of Morris Dees and the Southern Poverty Law Center."

19. "Our Society Is Strongest When We Stand against Bias and Inequity," Inclusion, Google, https://www.google.org/our-work/inclusion/.

20. Mark Pulliam, "A Demagogic Bully," City Journal, July 27, 2017, https://www.city-journal.org/html/demagogic-bully-15370.html.

21. Peter Hasson, "Prominent Christian Legal Group Barred from Amazon Program while Openly Anti-Semitic Groups Remain," Daily Caller, May 5, 2018, https://dailycaller.com/2018/05/05/amazon-smile-liberal-splc-anti-semitic-groups/.

22. Ibid.

23. "Center for Immigration Studies Files a Civil RICO Lawsuit against the President of the Southern Poverty Law Center," Litigation, Center for Immigration Studies, January 16, 2019, https://cis.org/Press-Release/CIS-RICO-Lawsuit-SPLC.

24. Peter Hasson, "The Left-Wing SPLC Is Now Policing What Music You Can Listen To on Spotify," Daily Caller, May 11, 2018, https://dailycaller.com/2018/05/11/splc-policing-music-on-spotify/.

25. Peter Hasson, "Exclusive: Facebook, Amazon, Google, and Twitter All Work with Left-Wing SPLC," Daily Caller, June 6, 2018, https://dailycaller.com/2018/06/06/splc-partner-google-facebook-amazon/.

26. Swathi Shanmugasundaram, "The Persistence of Anti-Muslim Hate on Facebook," Southern Poverty Law Center, May 5, 2018, https://www.splcenter.org/hatewatch/2018/05/05/persistence-anti-muslim-hate-facebook.

27. David Mikkelson, "UPOs Over Haiti," Fauxtography, Snopes, August 22, 2007, http://www.snopes.com/photos/odd/haitiufos.asp.

28. David Mikkelson, "The Young Family," Fauxtography, Snopes, May 6, 2005, http://www.snopes.com/photos/arts/family.asp

29. Peter Hasson, "Fact-Checking Snopes: Website's Political 'Fact-Checker' Is Just a Failed Liberal Blogger," Daily Caller, June 17, 2016, https://dailycaller.com/2016/06/17/fact-checking-snopes-websites-political-fact-checker-is-just-a-failed-liberal-blogger/.

30. Peter Hasson, "Snopes Caught Lying about Lack of American Flags at Democratic Convention," Daily Caller, July 28, 2016, https://dailycaller.com/2016/07/28/snopes-caught-lying-about-lack-of-american-flags-at-democratic-convention/.

31. Peter Hasson, "Snopes Caught Playing Defense for Democrats Who Sat during Navy SEAL Tribute," Daily Caller, March 2, 2017, https://dailycaller.com/2017/03/02/snopes-caught-playing-defense-for-democrats-who-sat-during-navy-seal-tribute/.

32. Peter Hasson, "Fact-Check: Snopes Gets Facts Wrong while Defending Planned Parenthood," Daily Caller, February 17, 2017," https://dailycaller.com/2017/02/17/fact-check-snopes-gets-facts-wrong-while-defending-planned-parenthood/.

33. Peter Hasson, "Snopes, Fact-Checker for Facebook and Google, Botches Fact Check," Daily Caller, December 6, 2018, https://dailycaller.com/2018/12/06/snopes-facebook-google-fact-check/.

34. Alex Pfeiffer and Peter Hasson, "Snopes, Which Will Be Fact-Checking for Facebook, Employs Leftists Almost Exclusively," Daily Caller, December 16, 2016, https://dailycaller.com/2016/12/16/snopes-facebooks-new-fact-checker-employs-leftists-almost-exclusively/.

35. Anders Hagstrom, "Facebook Used Snopes 'Fact Check' To Threateen Christian Satire Site by 'Mistake,'" Daily Caller, March 2, 2018, https://dailycaller.com/2018/03/02/facebook-snopes-fact-checks-demonitize-christian-satire/.

36. Peter Hasson, "Snopes, Fact-Checker for Facebook and Google, Botches Fact Check," Daily Caller, December 6, 2018, https://dailycaller.com/2018/12/06/snopes-facebook-google-fact-check/.

37. Jake Sherman (@JakeSherman), "Yeah, It's Not Really a Question. The Thing Was Nearly 100% Wrong," Twitter post, December 7, 2018, https://twitter.com/JakeSherman/status/1071055823135215616.

38. Peter Hasson, "Snopes Fact-Checker for Facebook and Google, Botches Nathan Phillips Fact Check," Daily Caller, January 24, 2019, https://dailycaller.com/2019/01/24/snopes-nathan-phillips-vietnam/.

39. Alana Goodman, "Native American Activist Nathan Phillips Has Violent Criminal Record and Escaped from Jail as Teenager," *Washington Examiner,* January 23, 2019, https://www.washingtonexaminer.com/politics/native-american-activist-nathan-phillips-has-violent-criminal-record-and-escaped-from-jail-as-teenager.

40. Peter Hasson, "Snopes Butchers Fact Check of Viral Smear of Chick-fil-A," Daily Caller, October 16, 2019, https://dailycaller.com/2019/10/16/chick-fil-a-uganda-fact-check/.

41. Ibid.

42. Ibid.

43. Peter Hasson, "What Ingraham, Sinclair, and Williamson Have in Common," Daily Caller, April 5, 2018, https://dailycaller.com/2018/04/05/kevin-williamson-laura-ingraham-sinclair-media-matters-boycott/.

44. Patrick Howley, "Media Matters Executive Wrote Racist, Anti-Semitic, Andi-'Tranny' Blog Posts," Daily Caller, October 6, 2014, https://dailycaller.com/2014/10/06/media-matters-executive-wrote-racist-anti-semitic-anti-tranny-blog-posts/.

45. Angelo Carusone, "Tranny Paradise," Rants, AngeloCarusone.com, November 14, 2005, http://web.archive.org/web/20060216022915/http://www.angelocarusone.com:80/.

46. Angelo Carusone, "Facebook Caves In to Pressure from Conservatives," CNN, June 26, 2018, https://www.cnn.com/2018/06/25/opinions/facebook-caves-to-conservatives-carusone/index.html.

47. Amber Athey, "CNN Silent on Contributor Fantasizing about Punching Covington Boy," Daily Caller, January 22, 2019, https://dailycaller.com/2019/01/22/cnn-bakari-sellers-punching-covington-nicholas-sandmann/.

48. Scot Morefield, "CNN's Symone Sanders Doubles Down after Being Criticized for Mocking Covington Student's TV Interview,"

Daily Caller, January 22, 2019, https://dailycaller.com/2019/01/22/cnn-symone-sanders-nick-sandmann-covington/.

49. Joe Schoffstall, "Media Matters: Force Policy Changes at Tech Companies To Fight 'Fake News,'" Free Beacon, April 19, 2018, https://freebeacon.com/issues/media-matters-force-policy-changes-tech-companies-fight-fake-news/.

50. Ibid.

51. Rachel Stoltzfoos, "Media Matters Offers Absurd Justifications for Right-Wing 'Extremists' List," Daily Caller, July 11, 2019, https://dailycaller.com/2019/07/11/media-matters-right-wing-extremists-list/.

52. Peter Hasson, "It Turns Out Alex Jones Is Just Pretending," Daily Caller, April 17, 2017, https://dailycaller.com/2017/04/17/it-turns-out-alex-jones-is-just-pretending/.

53. Mollie McHugh, "A Timeline of Vacillation: How Twitter Came To Suspend Alex Jones," The Ringer, August 16, 2018, https://www.theringer.com/tech/2018/8/16/17705492/a-timeline-of-vacillation-how-twitter-came-to-suspend-alex-jones.

54. "Twitter Bans Alex Jones and InfoWars; Cites Abusive Behavior," Media, NPR, Spetmber 6, 2018, https://www.npr.org/2018/09/06/645352618/twitter-bans-alex-jones-and-infowars-cites-abusive-behavior.

55. Sonny Bunch, "The Untenable Tension between Freedom of Speech and Freedom of Association," Washington Post, August 8, 2018, https://www.washingtonpost.com/news/act-four/wp/2018/08/08/the-untenable-tension-between-freedom-of-speech-and-freedom-of-association/?noredirect=on&utm_term=.506fa75ba1f3.

56. Brendan O'Neill, "Alex Jones and the Rise of Corporate Censorship," Spiked, August 7, 2018, https://www.spiked-online.com/2018/08/07/alex-jones-and-the-rise-of-corporate-censorship/#.W3DoXNhKjq1.

57. Francis Fukuyama, "Social Media and Censorship," American Interest, August 8, 2018, https://www.the-american-interest.com/2018/08/08/social-media-and-censorship/.

58. Chris Murphy (@ChrisMurphyCT), "Infowars Is the Tip of a Giant Iceberg of Hate and Lies That Uses Sites Like Facebook and YouTube To Tear Our Nation Apart. These Companies Must Do More," Twitter post, August 6, 2018, https://twitter.com/ChrisMurphyCT/status/1026580187784404994

59. Chris White, "Google Emplyees Are Mad YouTube Didn't Lower the Boom on Steven Crowder," Daily Caller, June 7, 2019, https://dailycaller.com/2019/06/07/youtube-steven-crowder-censor/.

60. David Krayden, "New Yorker Fact Checker Resigns after Falsely Accusing ICE Officer of Having Nazi Tattoo," Daily Caller, June 25, 2018, https://dailycaller.com/2018/06/25/new-yorker-fact-checker-resigns-ice-officer-tattoo/.

61. Ben Shapiro, "So, Here's a Giant List of All the Dumb Stuff I've Ever Done (Don't Worry, I'll Keep Updating It)," Daily Wire, July 20, 2018, https://www.dailywire.com/news/33362/so-heres-giant-list-all-dumb-stuff-ive-ever-done-ben-shapiro.

62. "Center for American Progress (CAP)," Non-Profit, Influence Watch, https://www.influencewatch.org/non-profit/center-for-american-progress-cap/.

63. "Adopt the Terms," Petition, Change the Terms, https://www.changetheterms.org/terms.

64. Ryan Mac, Joseph Bernstein, Charlie Warzel, and Mat Honan, "This Document Is Some of the Research Facebook Commissioned on George Soros," Tech, BuzzFeed.News, December 1, 2018, https://www.buzzfeednews.com/article/ryanmac/soros-facebook-definers-research.

65. "Search Results for 'Facebook *Weekly Standard*,'" Media Matters for America, https://www.mediamatters.org/facebook-weekly-standard.

66. William Saletan, "The *Weekly Standard's* Kavanaugh Fact Check Was Correct," Politics, Slate, September 12, 2018, https://slate.com/news-and-politics/2018/09/thinkprogress-weekly-standard-facebook-fact-check-kavanaugh.html.

Chapter Eight: The Narrative

1. Shiela Dang, "Google, Facebook Have Tight Grip on Growing U.S. Online Ad Market: Report," Reuters, June 5, 2019, https://www.reuters.com/article/us-alphabet-facebook-advertising/google-facebook-have-tight-grip-on-growing-u-s-online-ad-market-report-idUSKCN1T61IV.

2. Ibid.

3. Marc Tracy, "Google Made $4.7 Billion from the News Industry in 2018, Study Says," *New York Times*, June 9, 2019, https://www.nytimes.com/2019/06/09/business/media/google-news-industry-antitrust.html.

4. Mathew Ingram, "*NYT* Promotes Questionable Study on Google and the Media," June 10, 2019, https://www.cjr.org/the_new_gatekeepers/nyt-google-media.php.

5. Jack Shafer, "Newspapers' Embarrssing Lobbying Campaign," *Politico,* June 10, 2019, https://www.politico.com/magazine/story/2019/06/10/newspapers-embarrassing-lobbying-campaign-227100.

6. Jefferson Pooley and Michael Socolow, "The Myth of the *War of the Worlds* Panic," Slate, October 23, 2013, https://slate.com/culture/2013/10/orson-welles-war-of-the-worlds-panic-myth-the-infamous-radio-broadcast-did-not-cause-a-nationwide-hysteria.html.

7. Olivia Solon, "Facebook's Failure: Did Fake News and Polarized Politics Get Trump Elected?" *The Guardian,* November 10, 2016, https://www.theguardian.com/technology/2016/nov/10/facebook-fake-news-election-conspiracy-theories.

8. Max Read, "Donald Trump Won because of Facebook," *New York Magazine,* November 9, 2016, http://nymag.com/intelligencer/2016/11/donald-trump-won-because-of-facebook.html.

9. Brendan Nyhan, "Fake News and Bots May Be Worrisome but Their Political Power Is Overblown," *New York Times,* February 13, 2018, https://www.nytimes.com/2018/02/13/upshot/fake-news-and-bots-may-be-worrisome-but-their-political-power-is-overblown.html.

10. Peter Hasson, "Despite Media Freak-Out, Data Shows Fake News Sites Have Tiny Audience," Daily Caller, December 18, 2016, https://dailycaller.com/2016/12/18/despite-media-freak-out-data-shows-fake-news-sites-have-tiny-audience/.

11. Brendan Nyhan, "Why Fears of Fake News Are Overhyped," Gen. Medium.com, February 4, 2019, https://medium.com/s/reasonable-doubt/why-fears-of-fake-news-are-overhyped-2ed9ca0a52c9.

12. Peter Hasson, "Poll: Majority of Democrats Believe a Straight-Up Conspiracy Theory," Daily Caller, July 26, 2018, https://dailycaller.com/2018/07/26/democrats-russia-trump-election-poll/. Peter Hasson, "Alternate Reality: 58 Percent of Dems Think Russia Rigged Vote Count To Get Trump Elected," Daily Caller, May 31, 2017, https://dailycaller.com/2017/05/31/alternate-reality-58-percent-of-dems-think-russia-rigged-vote-count-to-get-trump-elected/.

13. Peter Hasson, "'We Don't Track Bots': What the Media's Russian Bot Coverage Is Getting All Wrong," Daily Caller, April 9, 2018, https://dailycaller.com/2018/04/09/hamilton-68-russian-bots-media-coverage/.

14. Ibid.

15. Chuck Ross, "Rump Supporter Says CNN Reporter 'Ambushed' Her in Interview about Russian Troll Group," Daily Caller, February 26, 2018, https://dailycaller.com/2018/02/26/drew-griffin-cnn-donald-trump-florida-robert-mueller/.

16. Justin Caruso, "Elderly Trump Supporter Woman Exposed to Vicious Harassment Following CNN Report," Daily Caller, February 21, 2018, https://dailycaller.com/2018/02/21/elderly-woman-cnn-threatened/.

17. Derek Hunter, "Michael Moore Participated in Russia-Sponsored Anti-Trump Rally," Daily Caller, February 19, 2018, https://dailycaller.com/2018/02/19/michael-moore-russian-anti-trump-rally/.

18. Peter Hasson, "Women's March Promoted Russian Propaganda," Daily Caller, October 23, 2017, https://dailycaller.com/2017/10/23/womens-march-promoted-russian-propaganda/.

19. Amber Athey, "Antifa Accused of Attacking Marines. CNN's Don Lemon and Chris Cuomo Once Excused Antifa Violence," Daily Caller, December 17, 2018, https://dailycaller.com/2018/12/17/antifa-hispanic-marines-cnn-don-lemon-chris-cuomo/.

20. Peter Hasson, "Iran Caught Using Fake Social Media Accounts To Push Anti-Trump, Pro-Bernie Propaganda," Daily Caller, August 22, 2018, https://dailycaller.com/2018/08/22/iran-fake-social-media-accounts/.

21. Kaitlyn Schallhorn, "North Dakota Democratic Party Discourages Hunters from Voting, Claims They Could Lose Out-of-State Licenses," Fox News, November 2, 2018, https://www.foxnews.com/politics/north-dakota-democratic-party-discourages-hunts-from-voting-claims-they-could-lose-out-of-state-licenses.

22. Peter Hasson, Joe Simonson, "If You Only Get Your News frm CNN, You Have No Idea This Story Happened," Daily Caller, December 27, 2018, https://dailycaller.com/2018/12/27/cnn-democrat-russian-false-flag/.

23. Benjamin Mullin and Deepa Seetharaman, "Publishing Executives Argue facebook Is Overly Deferential to Conservatives," *Wall Street Journal,*

July 17, 2018, https://www.wsj.com/articles/publishing-executives-argue-facebook-is-overly-deferential-to-conservatives-1531802201.

24. Peter Hasson, "Facebook Plans To 'Dial Up' Suppression of Certain News Outlets," Daily Caller, May 1, 2018, https://dailycaller.com/2018/05/01/facebook-newsfeed-trusted-sources-dial-up/.

25. Zach Carter, "Hey, Democrats: Pack the Court," HuffPost, June 29, 2018, https://www.huffingtonpost.com/entry/hey-democrats-pack-the-court_us_5b33f7a8e4b0b5e692f3f3d4.

26. Ibid.

27. Andrew Kerr, "How BuzzFeed's 'Data-Monster' Leveraged User Data To Fuel Super PACs, Target Voters," Daily Caller, May 6, 2018, https://dailycaller.com/2018/05/06/buzzfeeds-data-political-advertisements/.

28. Adam Johnson, "BuzzFeed's Obama Coverage Is 99 Percent Uncritical—and Borderline Creepy," Fair.org, June 30, 2016, https://fair.org/home/buzzfeeds-obama-coverage-is-99-percent-uncritical-and-borderline-creepy/.

29. Alex Pfeiffer, "The *Washington Post's* Incredibly Botched Story on 'Russian' Hacking," Daily Caller, January 3, 2017, https://dailycaller.com/2017/01/03/the-washington-posts-incredibly-botched-story-on-russian-hacking/.

30. Amber Athey, "CNN Walks Back Jeff Sessions-Russia Bombshell," Daily Caller, December 11, 2017, https://dailycaller.com/2017/12/11/cnn-walks-back-jeff-sessions-russia-bombshell/.

31. Amber Athey, "BuzzFeed's Trump Story Latest in Long List of Russia Bombshells That Weren't," Daily Caller, January 18, 2019, https://dailycaller.com/2019/01/18/buzzfeed-cohen-media-russia-bombshells/.

32. Peter Hasson, "Three CNN Employees Resign over Botched Trump-Russia Story," Daily Caller, June 26, 2017, https://dailycaller.com/2017/06/26/three-cnn-employees-resign-over-botched-trump-russia-story/.

33. Peter Hasson, "Yet Another Anonymously Sourced Trump-Russia Story Falls Apart," Daily Caller, September 7, 2017, https://dailycaller.com/2017/09/07/yet-another-anonymously-sourced-trump-russia-story-falls-apart/.

34. Ibid.

35. Athey, "BuzzFeed's Trump Story."

36. Amber Athey, "The Definitive List of Media Screw-Ups on the Trump-Russia Story," Daily Caller, May 3, 2018, https://dailycaller.com/2018/05/03/media-failure-russia-trump-story/.

37. Chuck Ross, "CNN Botches Major 'Bombshell' Alleging Contacts between Don Jr. and WikiLeaks," Daily Caller, December 8, 2017, https://dailycaller.com/2017/12/08/cnn-botches-major-bombshell-alleging-contacts-between-don-jr-and-wikileaks/.

38. Chuck Ross, "Mueller's Office Disputes BuzzFeed's Report," Daily Caller, January 18, 2019, https://dailycaller.com/2019/01/18/muellers-office-disputes-buzzfeeds-report/.

39. Amber Athey, "CNN and MSNBC Repeatedly Floated Impeachment over Disputed BuzzFeed Report," Daily Caller, January 18, 2019, https://dailycaller.com/2019/01/18/cnn-msnbc-impeach-trump-buzzfeed-mueller/.

40. Kieran Corcoran, "The Author of the Explosive New Trump Book Says He Can't Be Sure if Parts of It Are True," *Business Insider,* January 5, 2018, https://www.businessinsider.com/michael-wolff-note-says-he-doesnt-know-if-trump-book-is-all-true-2018-1.

41. Marty Steinberg, "Miachel Wolff's 'Fire and Fur': Some of the Facts Just Don't Stack Up," CNBC, January 7, 2018, https://www.cnbc.com/2018/01/07/michael-wolffs-fire-and-fury-some-of-the-facts-just-dont-stack-up.html.

42. "Trump: Bannon Has 'Lost His Mind,' Has No Influence in White House; Book: Bannon Calls Trump Tower Meeting 'Treasonous,'" CNN Newsroom, aired January 3, 2018, http://transcripts.cnn.com/TRANSCRIPTS/1801/03/cnr.05.html.

43. "New Book Raises Questions on Trump's Mindset; December Jobs Report Posted 148,000; The Trump Russia Investigation," CNN Newsroom, aired on January 5, 2018, http://transcripts.cnn.com/TRANSCRIPTS/1801/05/nday.06.html.

44. Peter Hasson, "Matt Drudge Slams Michael Wolff's 'Fabricated Bull****t'—Trump in 'Fine Form,'" Daily Caller, January 23, 2018, https://dailycaller.com/2018/01/23/matt-drudge-donald-trump-michael-wolff-fire-and-fury/.

45. "Explosive book Outlines Bannon-Kushner Rivalry," CNN Newsroom, aired on January 5, 2018, http://transcripts.cnn.com/TRANSCRIPTS/1801/05/nday.02.html.

46. A. J. Katz, "2018 Ratings: MSNBC Was the Only Top 25 Cable Network To Post Double-Digit Audience Growth," AdWeek.com, January 2, 2019, https://www.adweek.com/tvnewser/2018-ratings-msnbc-was-the-only-top-25-cable-network-to-post-double-digit-audience-growth/387956.

47. Julia Nista, "Scarborough Says Wolff's Claims about Trump in New Book 'Ring True,'" Daily Caller, January 4, 2018, https://dailycaller.com/2018/01/04/scarborough-says-wolffs-claim-about-trump-in-new-book-ring-true/.

48. David Rutz, "Media is Cool with Fake but Accurate 'Fire and Fury,'" Free Beacon, January 9, 2018, https://freebeacon.com/politics/media-cool-fake-accurate-fire-fury/.

49. Ibid.

Chapter Nine: What Comes Next

1. Von Georg Mascolo and Britta von der Heide, "1200 Frauen Wurden Opfer von Silvester-Gewalt," *Süddeutsche Zeitung*, July 10, 2016, https://www.sueddeutsche.de/politik/uebergriffe-in-koeln-frauen-wurden-opfer-von-silvester-gewalt-1.3072064.

2. Kirchick, James. *The End of Europe: Dictators, Demagogues, and the Coming Dark Age*, Kindle Edition, (New Haven: Yale University Press, 2017), Kindle locations 2229–2235.

3. Philip Oltermann and Pádraig Collins, "Two Members of Germany's Far-Right Party Investigated by State Prosecutor," *The Guardian*, January 2, 2018, https://www.theguardian.com/world/2018/jan/02/german-far-right-mp-investigated-anti-muslim-social-media-posts.

4. Chase Winter, "AfD Politician 'Censored' under New German Hate Speech Law for Anti-Muslim Tweet," DW.com, January 2, 2018, https://www.dw.com/en/afd-politician-censored-under-new-german-hate-speech-law-for-anti-muslim-tweet/a-41992679.

5. Rick Noack, "Leaked Document Says 2,000 Men Allegedly Assaulted 1,200 German Women on New Year's Eve," *Washington Post,* July 10, 2016, https://www.washingtonpost.com/news/worldviews/wp/2016/07/10/leaked-document-says-2000-men-allegedly-assaulted-1200-german-women-on-new-years-eve/?noredirect=on.

6. Riham Alkoussa, "Violent Crime Rises in Germany and Is Attributed to Refugees," Reuters, January 3, 2018, https://www.reuters.com/article/

us-europe-migrants-germany-crime/violent-crime-rises-in-germany-and-is-attributed-to-refugees-idUSKBN1ES16J.

7. David Martin, "German Satire Magazine *Titanic* back on Twitter Following 'Hate Speech' Ban," DW.com, January 6, 2018 ,https://www.dw.com/en/german-satire-magazine-titanic-back-on-twitter-following-hate-speech-ban/a-42046485

8. Justin Tallis, "German 'Facebook Law' Creates Risk of Over-Blocking," Reporters without Borders for Freedom of Information, July 10, 2017, https://rsf.org/en/news/german-facebook-law-creates-risk-over-blocking.

9. Jonah Shepp, "Angela Merkel Won Reelection, but Is She Still the Leader of the Free World," Intelligencer, September 25, 2017, http://nymag.com/intelligencer/2017/09/is-angela-merkel-still-the-leader-of-the-free-world.html?gtm=top&gtm=top.

10. Ewan Palmer, "YouTuber Count Dankula Who Taught Dog Nazi Salute Faces Jail for Hate Crime," *Newsweek,* March, 20, 2018, https://www.newsweek.com/youtuber-count-dankula-who-taught-dog-nazi-salute-faces-jail-hate-crime-853470.

11. "PF v. Mark Meechan," Judgements and Sentences, Judiciary of Scotland, April 23, 2018, http://www.scotland-judiciary.org.uk/8/1962/PF-v-Mark-Meechan.

12. Ibid.

13. "Woman Guilty of 'Racist' Snap Dogg Rap Lyric Instagram Post," BBC, April 19, 2018, https://www.bbc.com/news/uk-england-merseyside-43816921.

14. "Teenage Sentenced for Racist Instagram Post," News, Crown Prosecution Service, April 20, 2018, https://www.cps.gov.uk/mersey-cheshire/news/teenager-sentenced-racist-instagram-post.

15. "Woman Guilty of 'Racist' Snap Dogg Rap Lyric Instagram Post," BBC, April 19, 2018, https://www.bbc.com/news/uk-england-merseyside-43816921.

16. "Home Secretary Announces New National Online Hate Crime Hub," Press Release, Home Office, October 8, 2017, https://www.gov.uk/government/news/home-secretary-announces-new-national-online-hate-crime-hub.

17. Charlie Parker, "Police Arresting Nine People a Day in Fight against Web Trolls," *The Times,* October 12, 2017 https://www.thetimes.co.uk/article/police-arresting-nine-people-a-day-in-fight-against-web-trolls-b8nkpgp2d.

18. Ibid.

19. South Yorkshire Police (@syptweet), "In Addition to Reporting Hate Crime, Please Report Non-Crime Hate Incidents, Which Can Include Things Like Offensive or Insulting Comments, online, in Person," Twitter post, September 9, 2018, https://twitter.com/syptweet/status/1038891067381350401.

20. Martin Beckford, "Mother, 38, Is Arrested in Front of Her Children and Locked in a Cell for Seven HOURS after Calling a Transgender Woman a Man on Twitter," *Daily Mail,* February 10, 2019, https://www.dailymail.co.uk/news/article-6687123/Mother-arrested-children-calling-transgender-woman-man.html.

21. Lucy Bannerman, "*Father Ted* Writer Graham Linehan Says the Trans Activist Stephanie Hayden Is Dangerous Troll," *The Times,* September 29, 2018, https://www.thetimes.co.uk/article/father-ted-writer-graham-linehan-says-the-trans-activist-stephanie-hayden-is-dangerous-troll-6pwrg9p68.

22. Martin Beckford, "Mother, 38, Is Arrested in Front of Her Children."

23. Ibid.

24. "Man Complains of 'Orwellian Police' after Tweet Investigation," BBC, January 25, 2019, https://www.bbc.com/news/uk-england-humber-47005937.

25. James Kirkup, "Why Are the Police Stopping a 74-Year-Old Tweeting about Transgenderism?" Coffee House, *The Spectator,* February 5, 2019, https://blogs.spectator.co.uk/2019/02/why-are-the-police-stopping-a-74-year-old-tweeting-about-transgenderism/.

26. Margaret Nelson, "Death Doesn't Misgender. You Die as You Were Born," Dead Interesting Blog, January 19, 2018, https://deadinteresting.blogspot.com/2018/01/death-doesnt-misgender-you-die-as-you.html.

27. Lucy Powell, "Why I Am Seeking To Stamp Our Online Echo Chambers of Hate," *The Guardian,* September 10, 2018, https://amp.theguardian.com/technology/commentisfree/2018/sep/10/online-echo-chambers-hate-facebook-bill.

28. Mark Zuckerberg (@Mark Zuckerberg), "I Want To Share Some Thoughts on Facebook and the Election. Our Goal Is To Give Every Person a Voice. We Believe Deeply in People. Assuming That People Understand What Is

Important in Their Lives," Facebook post, November 12, 2016, https://www.facebook.com/zuck/posts/10103253901916271.

29. Sarah Jeong, "Nigel Farage Thinks Facebook Is Censoring Conservatives," The Verge, May 22, 2018, https://www.theverge.com/2018/5/22/17380972/nigel-farage-facebook-censoring-conservative-brexit-european-parliament-zuckerberg.

30. Brian Love and Jean-Baptiste Vey, "France To Get Tougher on Social Media Hate Speech-PM," Reuters, March 19, 2018, https://www.reuters.com/article/france-racism-socialmedia/france-to-get-tougher-on-social-media-hate-speech-pm-idUSL8N1R14G0.

31. Mathieu Rosemain, Michel Rose, Gwénaëlle Barzic, "France To 'Embed' Regulators at Facebook To Combat Hate Speech," Reuters, November 12, 2018, https://www.reuters.com/article/us-france-facebook-macron/france-to-embed-regulators-at-facebook-to-combat-hate-speech-idUSKCN1NH1UK.

32. Mark Scott and Zachary Young, "France and Facebook Announce Partnership against Online Hate Speech," Politico, November 12, 2018, https://www.politico.eu/article/emmanuel-macron-mark-zuckberg-paris-hate-speech-igf/.

33. Daniel Boffey, "EU Threatens To Crack Down on Facebook over Hate Speech," The Guardian, April 11, 2018, https://www.theguardian.com/technology/2018/apr/11/eu-heavy-sanctions-online-hate-speech-facebook-scandal.

34. "Facebook Is Doing Much Better at Removing Hate Speech, Says EU," MIT Technology Review, February 4, 2019, https://www.technologyreview.com/the-download/612878/facebook-is-doing-much-better-at-removing-hate-speech-says-the-eu/.

35. Anna Mitchell and Larry Diamond, "China's Surveillance State Should Scare Everyone," The Atlantic, February 2, 2018, https://www.theatlantic.com/international/archive/2018/02/china-surveillance/552203/.

36. Echo Huang, "China Is Investigating Its Internet Giants over Failures To Police Content—and Sending a Warning," Bad Information, Quartz, August 11, 2017, https://qz.com/1051539/china-is-investigating-its-internet-giants-tencent-tcehy-baidu-bidu-sina-weibo-wb-over-failures-to-police-content/.

37. "Tencent WeChat, Sina Weibo, Baidu Post Bar Are Suspected of Violating the 'Network Security Law' and Being Investigated," Cyberspace Administration of China, August 11, 2017, http://www.cac.gov.cn/2017-08/11/c_1121467425.htm.

38. Echo Huang, "China's Social Media Giants Want Their Users To Help Out with the Crushing Burden of Censorship," Quartz, January 5, 2018, https://qz.com/1172536/chinas-social-media-giants-tencent-toutiao-weibo-want-their-users-to-help-out-with-censorship/.

39. Zheping Huang, "All the Things You Can—and Can'tDo with Your WeChat Account in China," Double-Edged Sword, Quartz, December 28, 2017, https://qz.com/1167024/all-the-things-you-can-and-cant-do-with-your-wechat-account-in-china/.

40. Raymond Zhong, "A Saucy App Knows China's Taste in News. The Censors Are Worried," *New York Times,* January 2, 2018, https://www.nytimes.com/2018/01/02/business/china-toutiao-censorship.html.

41. Ibid.

42. Ryan Gallagher, "Leaked Transcript of Private Meeting Contradicts Google's Official Story on China," The Intercept, October 9, 2018, https://theintercept.com/2018/10/09/google-china-censored-search-engine/.

43. Ryan Gallagher and Lee Fang, "Google Suppresses Memo Revealing Plans To Closely Track Search Users in China," The Intercept, September 21, 2018, https://theintercept.com/2018/09/21/google-suppresses-memo-revealing-plans-to-closely-track-search-users-in-china/.

44. Kate Conger, "Google Removes 'Don't Be Evil' Clause from Its Code of Conduct," Gizmodo, May 18, 2018, https://gizmodo.com/google-removes-nearly-all-mentions-of-dont-be-evil-from-1826153393.

45. Nathan Halverson, "Facebook Knowingly Duped Game-Playing Kids and Their Parents out of Money," Reveal, Center for Investigative Reporting, January 24, 2019, https://www.revealnews.org/article/facebook-knowingly-duped-game-playing-kids-and-their-parents-out-of-money/.

46. Ibid.

47. Allum Bokhari, "Microsoft Teams with Establishment 'Newsguard' To Create News Blacklist," Breitbart, January 23, 2019, https://www.breitbart.com/tech/2019/01/23/microsoft-teams-with-establishment-newsguard-to-create-news-blacklist/.

48. Ibid.
49. Adrian Chen, "The Fake-News Fallacy," *New Yorker,* August 28, 2017, https://www.newyorker.com/magazine/2017/09/04/the-fake-news-fallacy.
50. Richard Pan, "Senate Bill 1424, Amended Version," California State Legislature, April 26, 2018, https://leginfo.legislature.ca.gov/faces/billTextClient.xhtml?bill_id=201720180SB1424.
51. Richard Pan, "SB 1424," Senate Rules Committee, August 28, 2018, https://www.scribd.com/document/438477789/20172018 0SB1424-Senate-Floor-Analyses.
52. Pan, "Senate Bill 1424, Amended Version."
53. Jimmy Gomez, "Assembly Bill 155, "California State Legislature, January 11, 2017, https://leginfo.legislature.ca.gov/faces/billNavClient.xhtml?bill_id=201720180AB155.
54. Matt Taibbi, "Taibbi: Beware the Slippery Slope of Facebook Censorship," *Rolling Stone,* August 2, 2018, https://www.rollingstone.com/politics/politics-features/facebook-censor-alex-jones-705766/.
55. Michael Tomasky, "Democrats, Crack the Whip on Facebook and Don't Hold Back When You Do It," Daily Beast, November 15, 2018, https://www.thedailybeast.com/democrats-crack-the-whip-on-facebook-and-dont-hold-back-when-ya-do-it.
56. Nina Jancowicz, "It's Time To Start Regulating Facebook," *Washington Post,* November 15, 2018, https://www.washingtonpost.com/news/democracy-post/wp/2018/11/15/its-time-to-start-regulating-facebook/?noredirect=on&utm_term=.9e98960a1bc2.

Chapter Ten: What to Do

1. Amber Athey, "Daily Caller Editor in Chief Locked Out of Account for Tweeting 'Learn To Code,'" Daily Caller, February 6, 2019, https://dailycaller.com/2019/02/06/daily-caller-twitter-locked-learn-to-code/.
2. Associated Press, "Bob Costas Pushes Gun Control on Air," NFL, ESPN.com, December 3, 2012, http://www.espn.com/nfl/story/_/id/8706492/bob-costas-advocates-gun-control-halftime.

Index